The joy *of* Origami

Yukiko Kurosava

Priority Publications

Fifth Reprint 2016

ISBN 978 81 8022 067 8

Published by Priority Publications
info@dspublishers.com
www.dspublishers.com

Cover Designed by White Mice Media

Printed in India at EIH Ltd. (Unit : Printing Press)
An Oberoi Group Company

Follow the instructions carefully before you start paper folding.

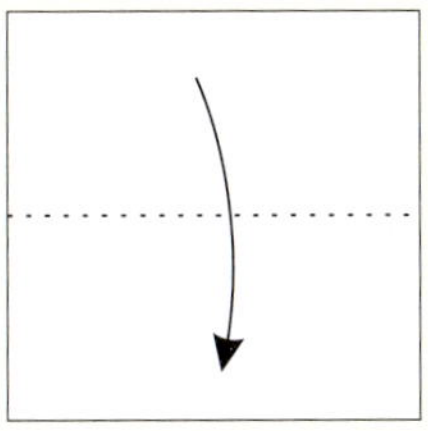

Fold in front....

.... like this.

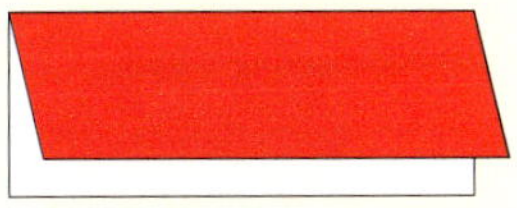

Valley fold (a series of dashes)

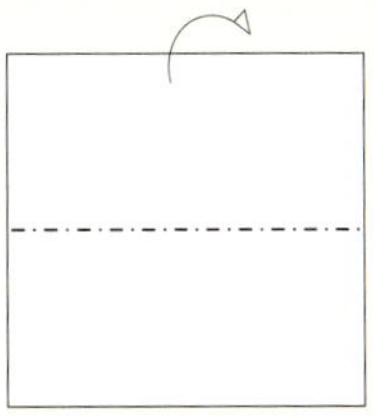

Fold behind....

.... like this.

Mountain Fold (a series of dashes and dots)

Stair-step Fold

This fold is made by combining a Valley Fold and a Mountain Fold to form a kind of pleat or stair-step....

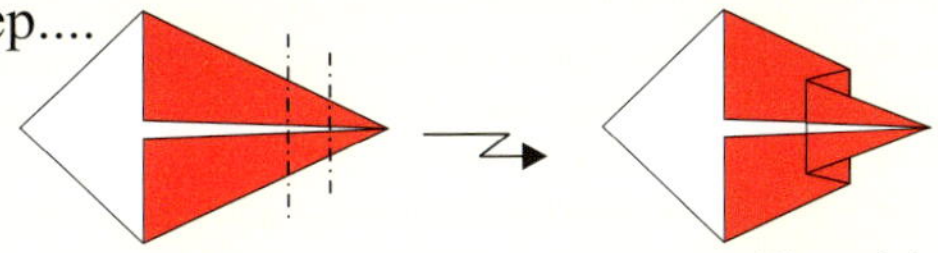

.... like this.

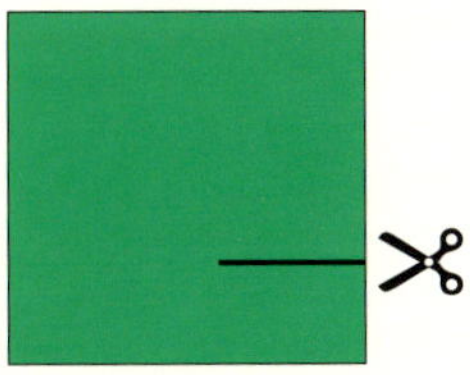

Cut

.... like this.

Fold over and over (like a flattened roll)....

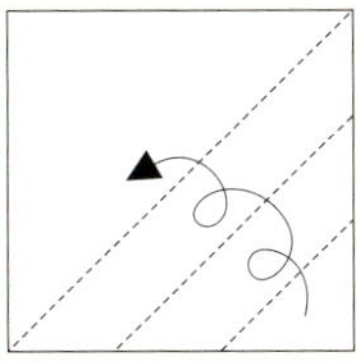

.... like this.

Enlarge

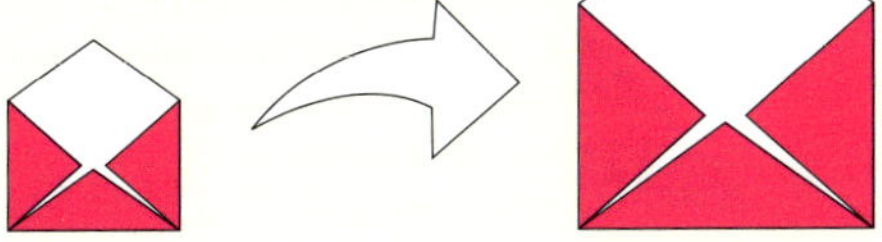

A swollen arrow indicates that next diagram is enlarged.

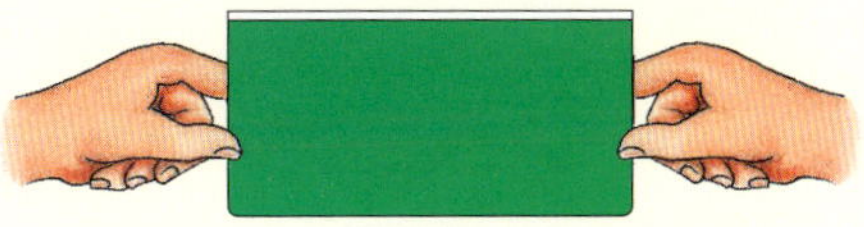

Neatly bring the corners together to coincide exactly.

Turn the model over.... .... like this.

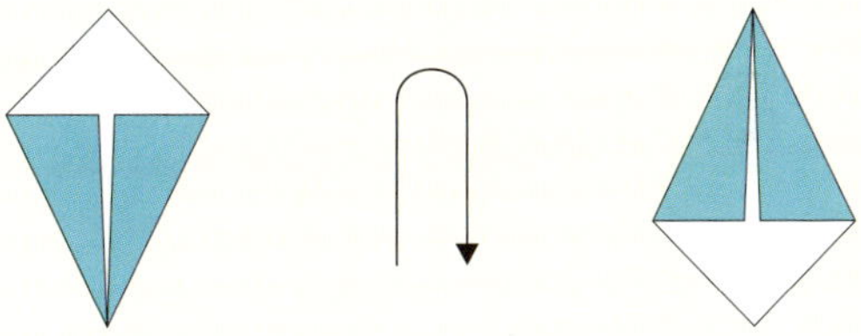

Turn upside down...... .... like this.

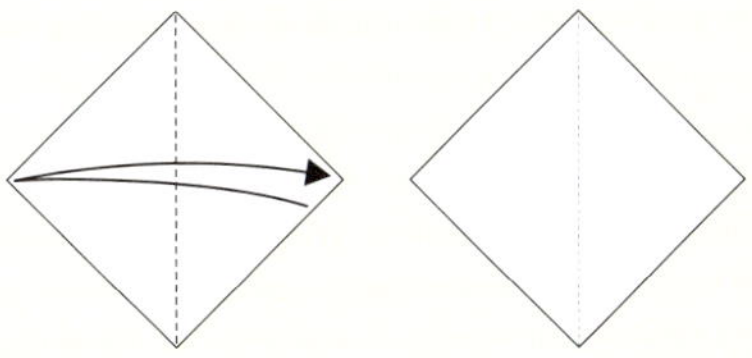

Fold and unfold to make a crease .... like this.

A faint line represents an existing crease line, or one which is the result of a previous step.

Inflate

This "Puff" arrow shows you where to blow.

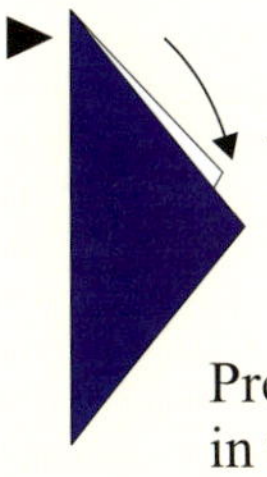

Apply force

Press or push in the required direction.

To sharpen the crease, use the finger-nail and the thumb-nail as shown in the diagram.

Learn to make good Squash Fold, Pocket Fold and Hood Fold.

Squash Fold

1
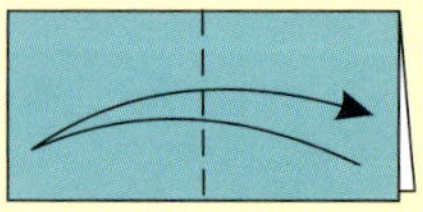
Fold in half and unfold.

2
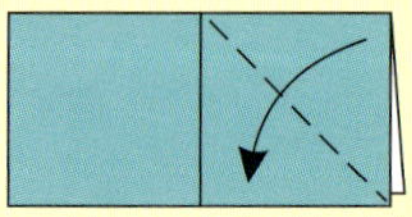
Fold the top right corner forward and backward and then unfold.

3
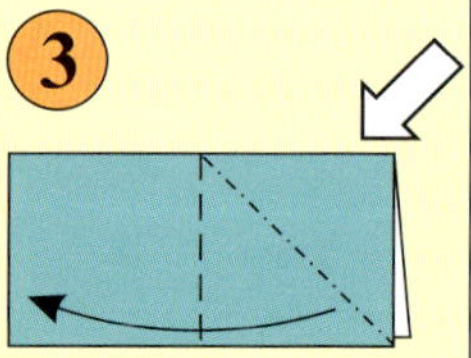
Press the top right corner at its upper edge....

4
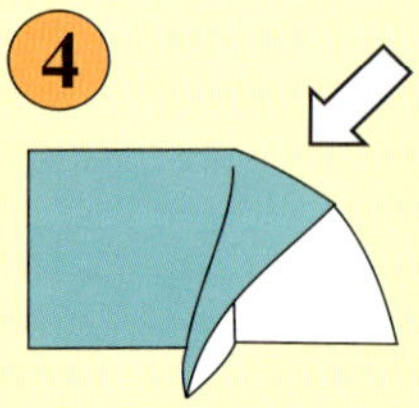
.... to open out into a triangle when flattened....

5
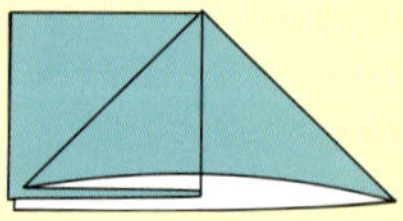
.... like this.

This is a **Squash Fold**.

Pocket Fold

1
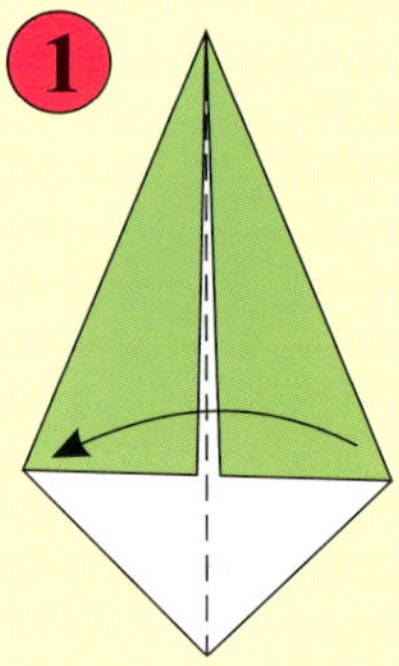
Fold in half from right to left.

2
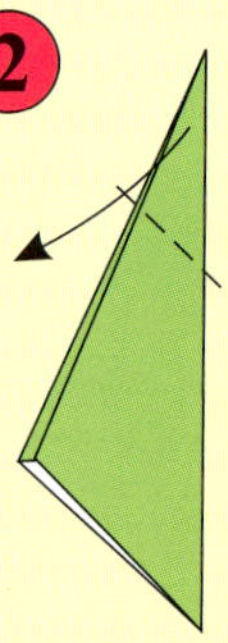
Fold the top corner forward and backward and unfold it.

3
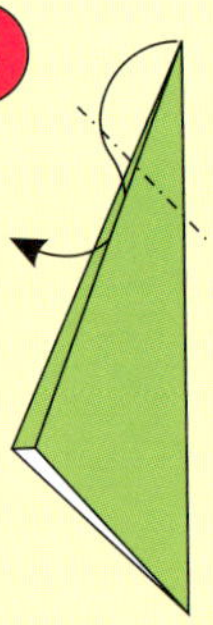
Now fold the top corner at the crease to bring it down between the two layers of the paper....

4

.... reversing its middle crease....

5

… like this.

This is a **Pocket Fold**.

Hood Fold

1
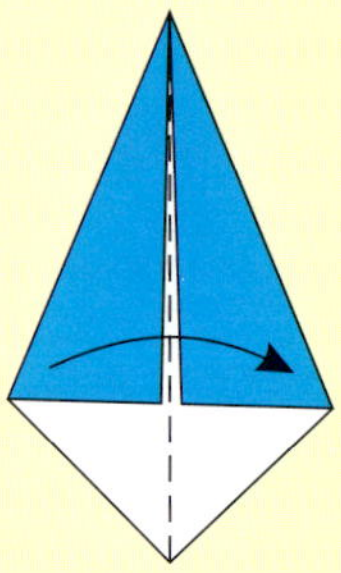
Fold in half from left to right.

2
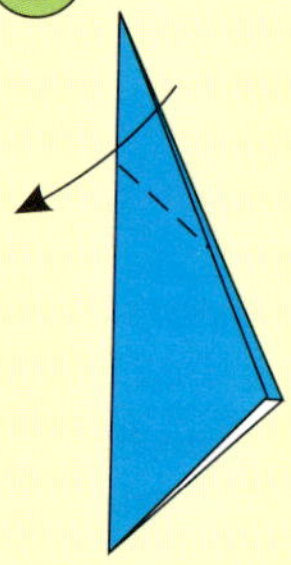
Fold the top corner forward and backward and unfold.

3

Now, fold the top corner at the crease inside out by slightly opening the flaps....

4
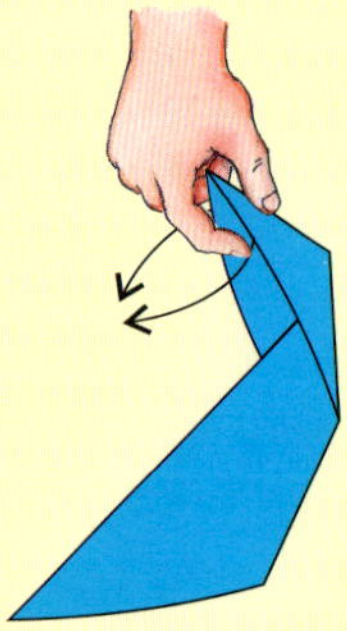
....like this.

5
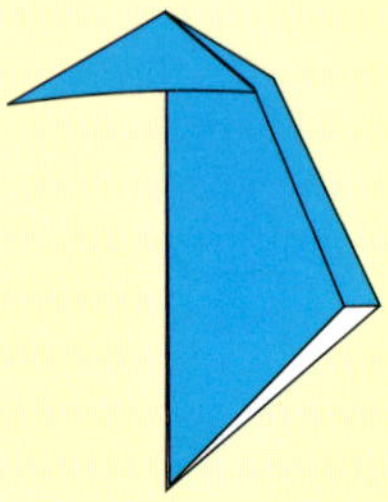
This is a **Hood Fold**.

Contents

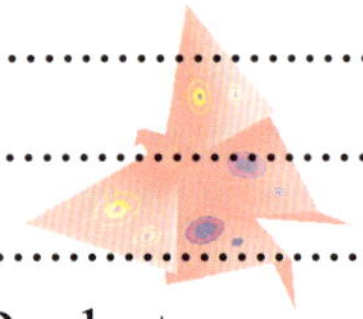
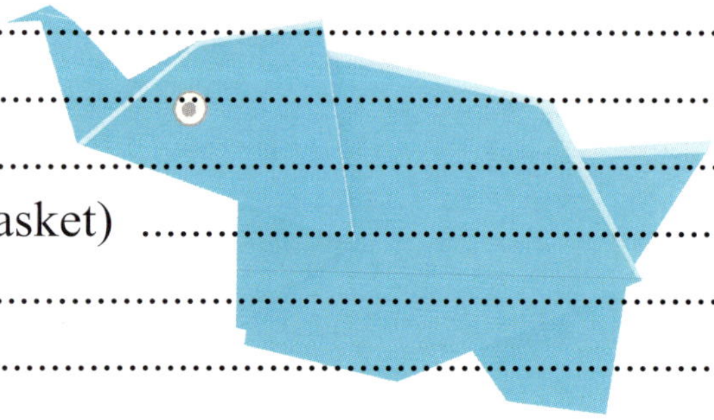
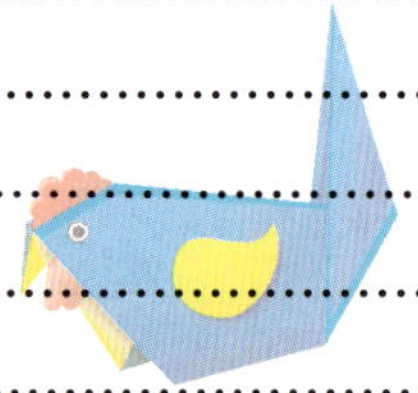

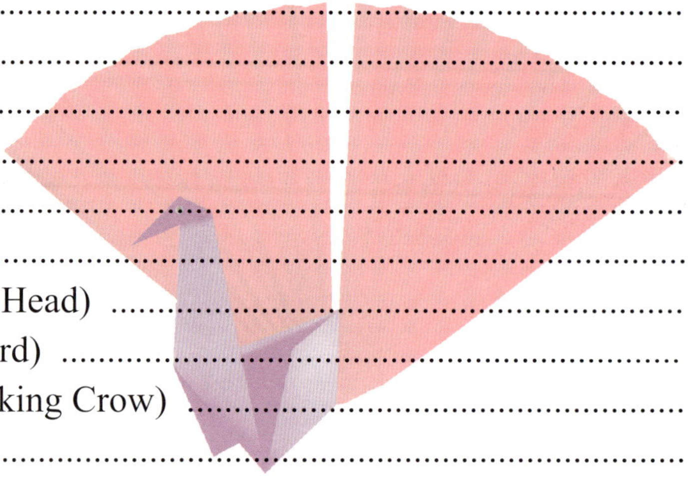

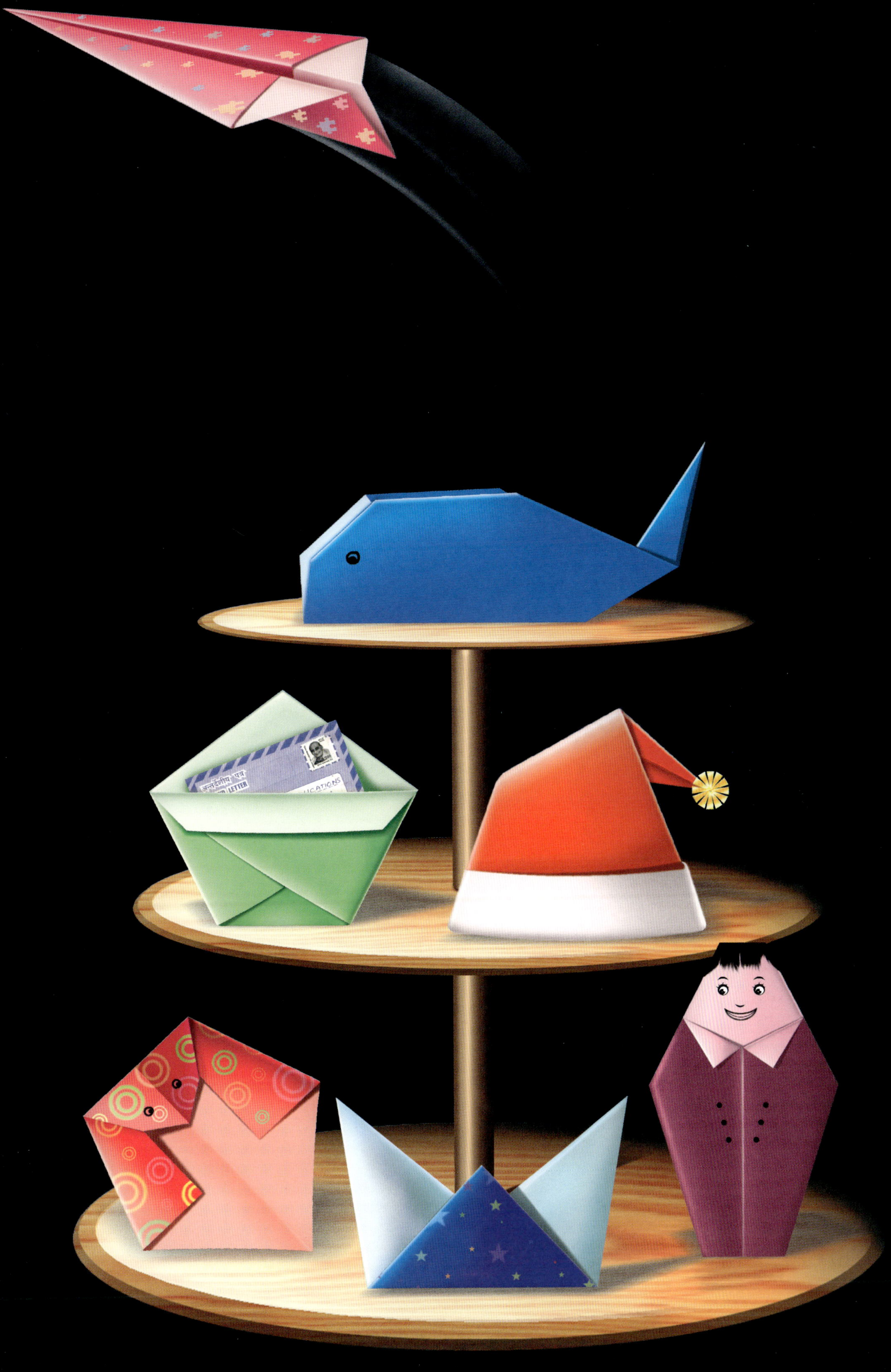

Owl

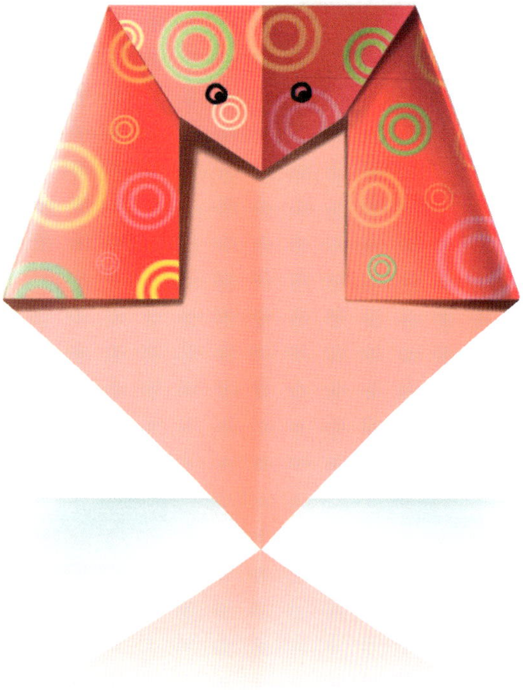

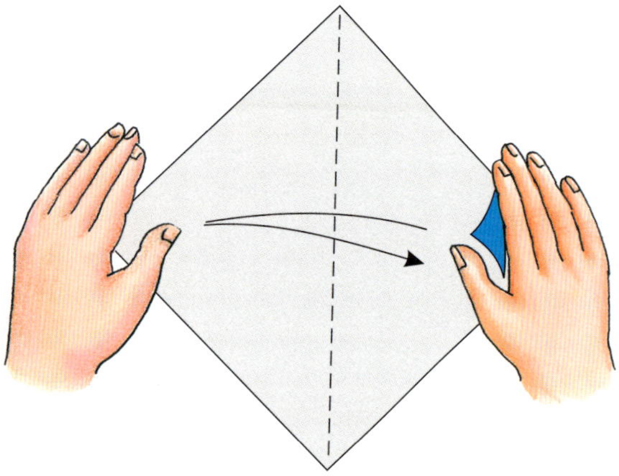

1 Fold and then unfold along the dotted line to make a crease.

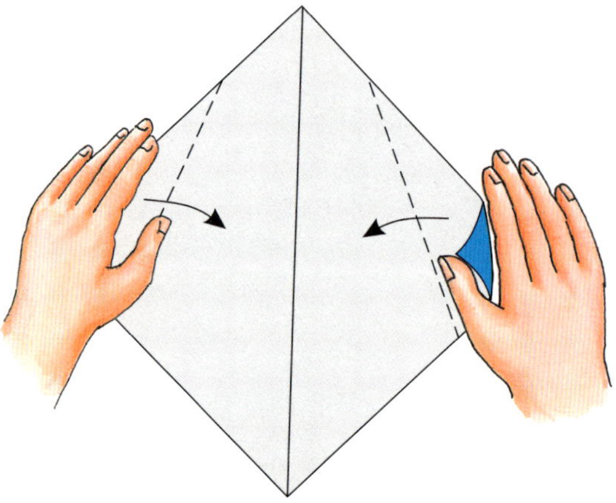

2 Fold the right and left corners along the dotted lines.

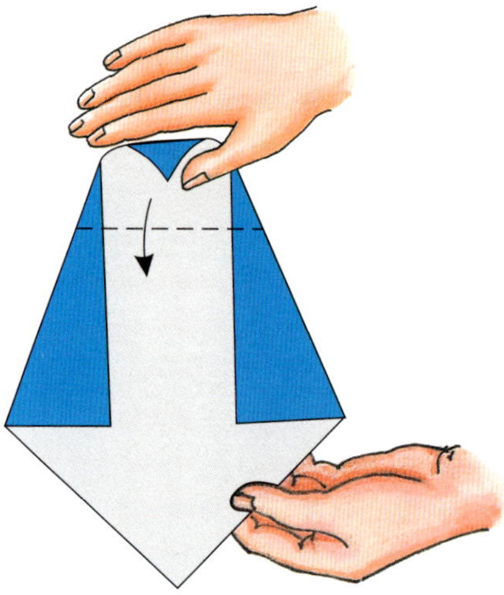

3 Fold the top corner downward along the dotted line.

Draw the eyes ....

4 ..... like this.

Aeroplane

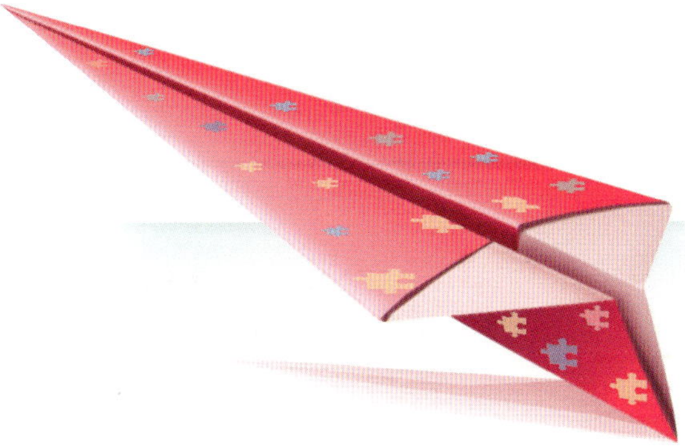

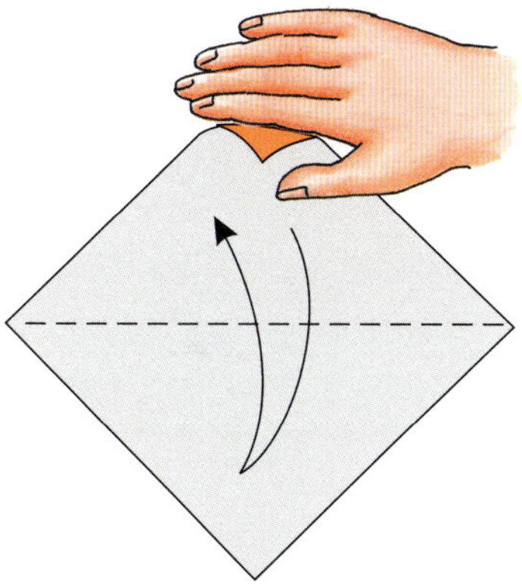

1 Fold and unfold along the dotted line.

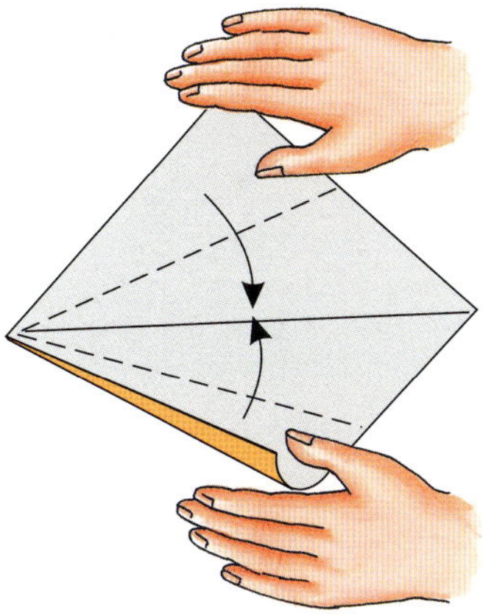

2 Fold both the sides to the centre line along the dotted lines.

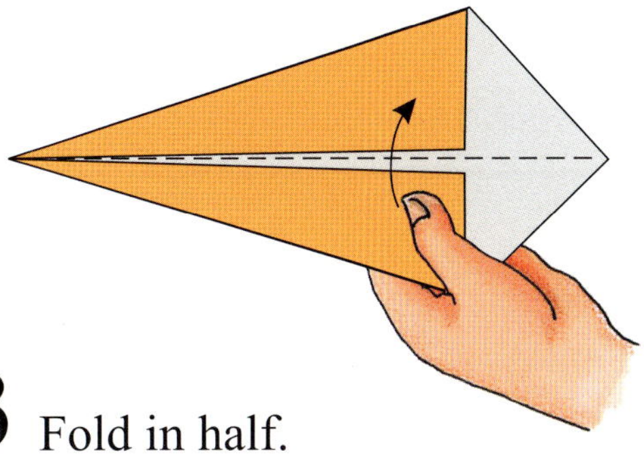

3 Fold in half.

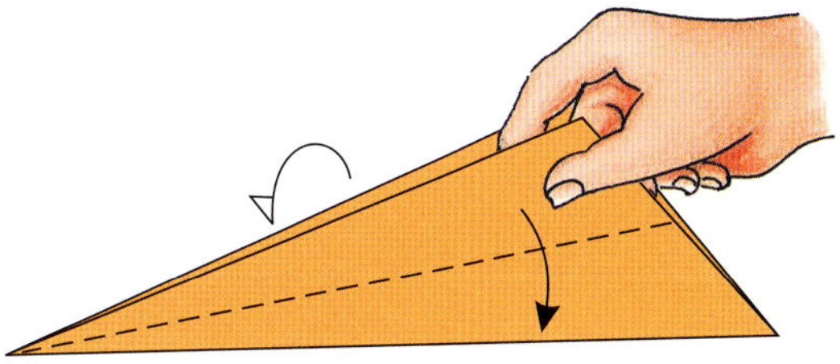

4 Now fold both the sides along the dotted lines outwards....

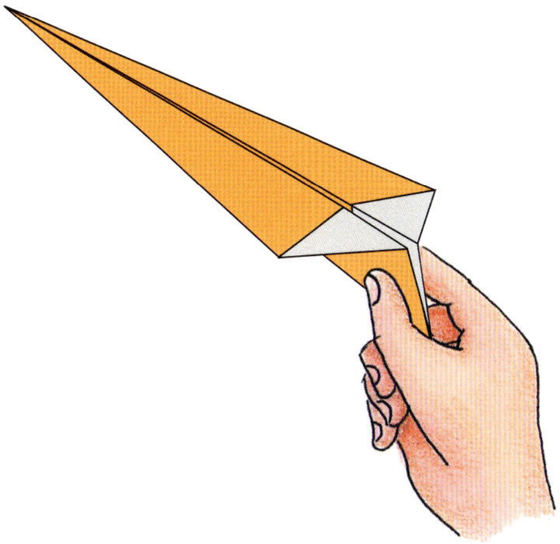

5 .... and your aeroplane is ready to fly.

Crown

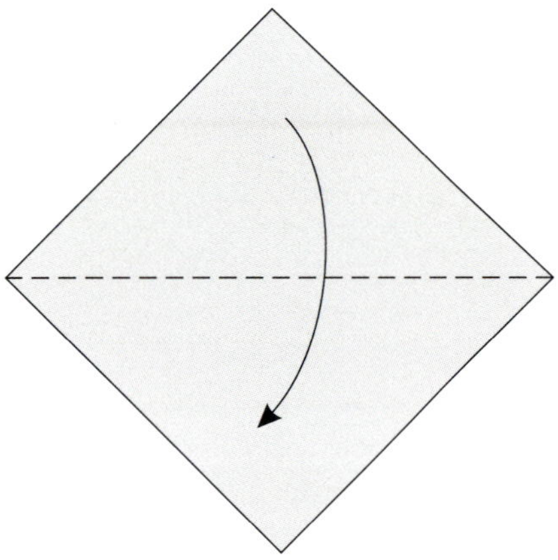

1 Fold along the dotted line as shown.

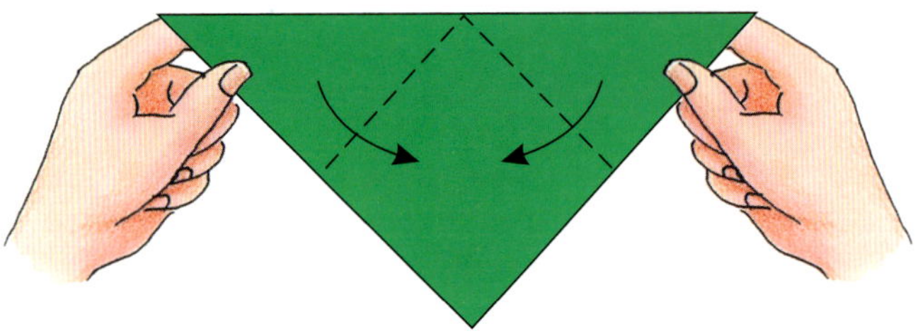

2 Fold the left and right corners down to meet the bottom point.

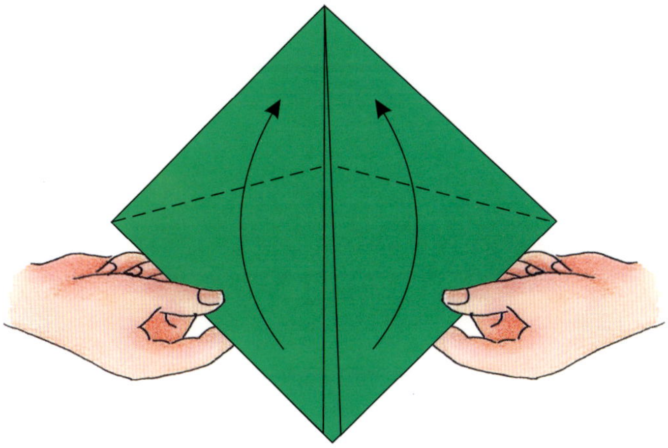

3 Fold upwards along the dotted lines.

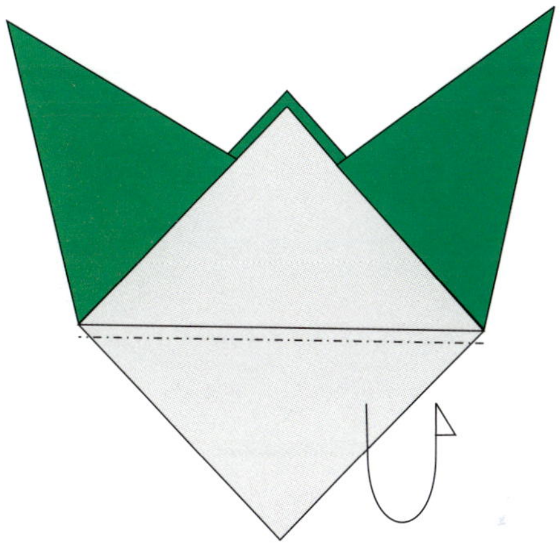

5 Now use a mountain fold to fold the back flap upwards.

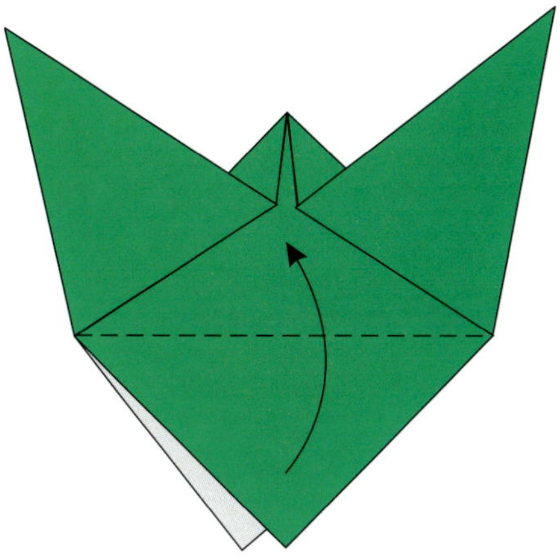

4 Fold the front flap upwards using a valley fold.

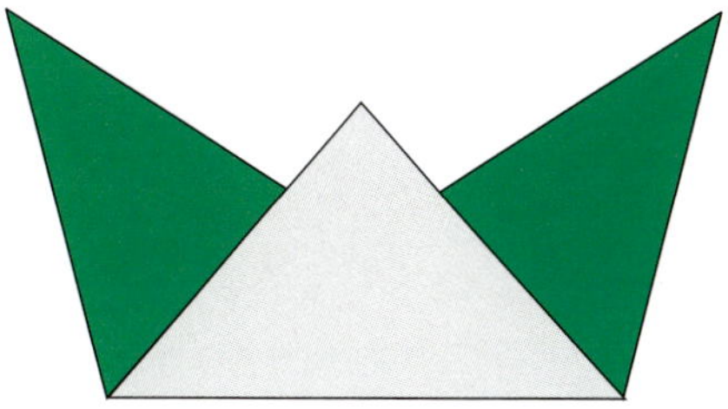

6 Your crown is ready.

Doll

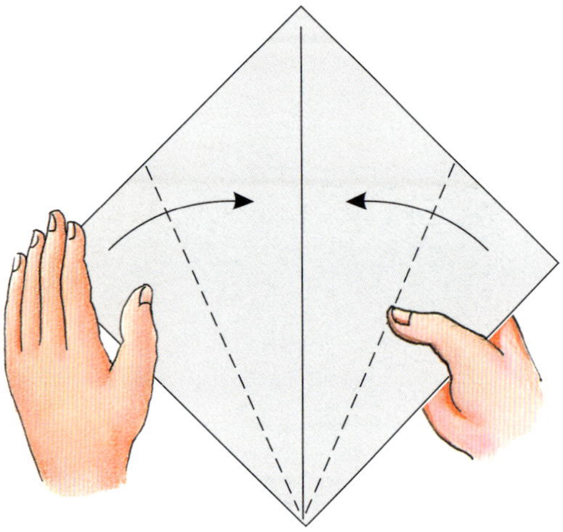

1 Fold in half and unfold it. Fold the left and right corners to the centre line.

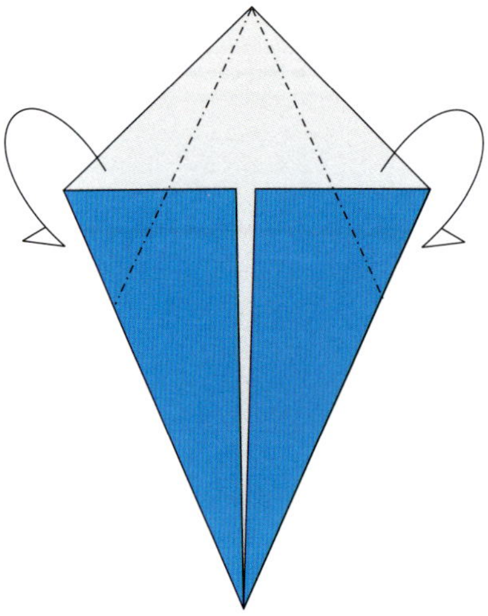

2 Fold the left and right corners backwards along the dotted lines.

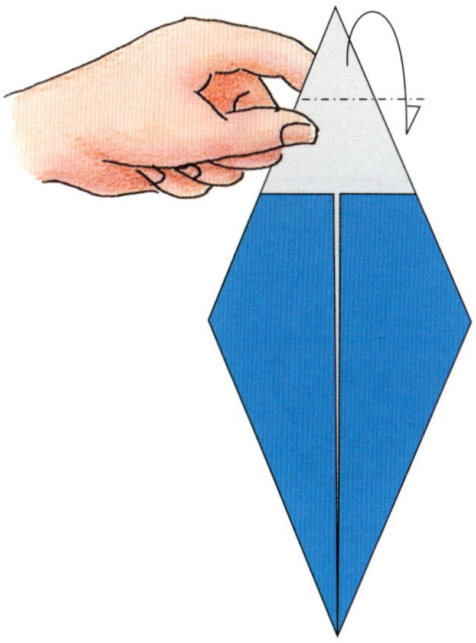

3 Fold the upper tip backwards.

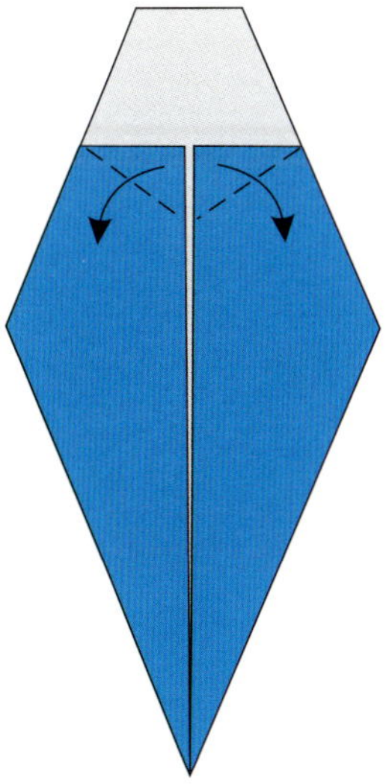

4 Fold the corners of the flaps to form collars of her dress.

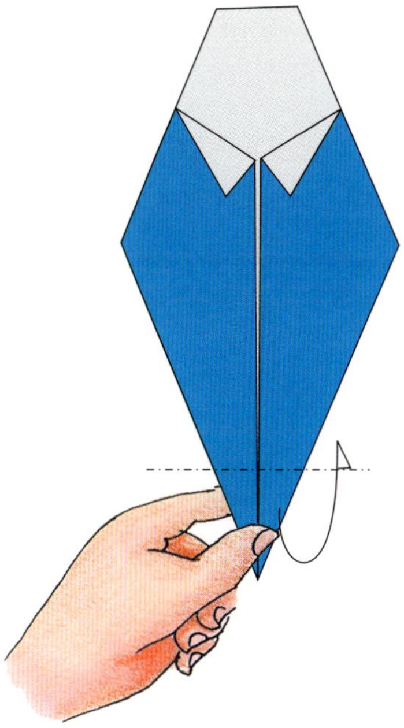

5 Fold the lower tip backwards along the dotted line.

6 Use a pen to draw her hair, eyes, mouth and the buttons of her dress.

Santa's Cap

1 Fold upward one after another along the dotted lines....

2 .... like this.

3 Fold the right and left corners in such a manner that they slightly overlap.

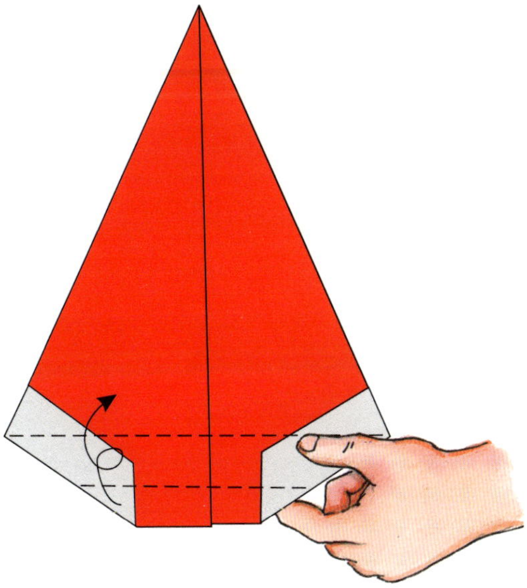

4 Fold upward twice along the dotted lines.

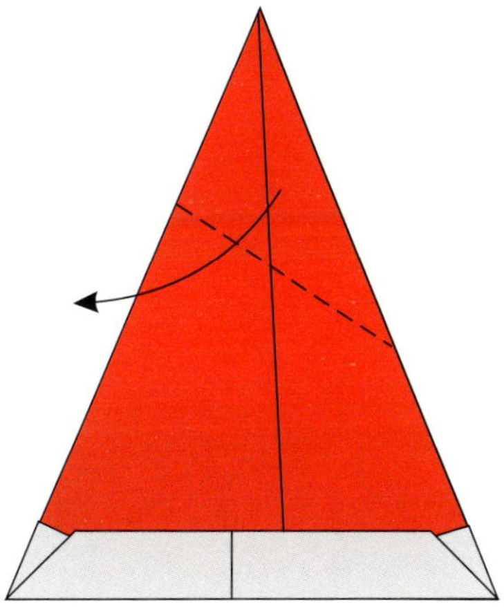

5 Fold the top corner in the direction of the arrow.

6 Paste a paper flower at the tip of the cap.

Letter Rack

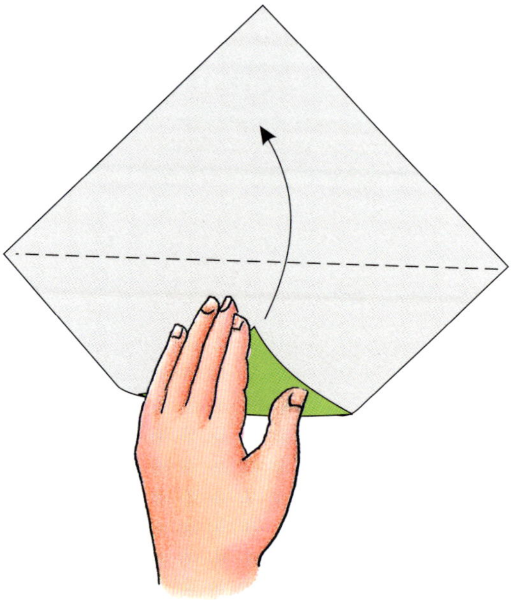

1 Fold along the dotted line in the direction of arrow.

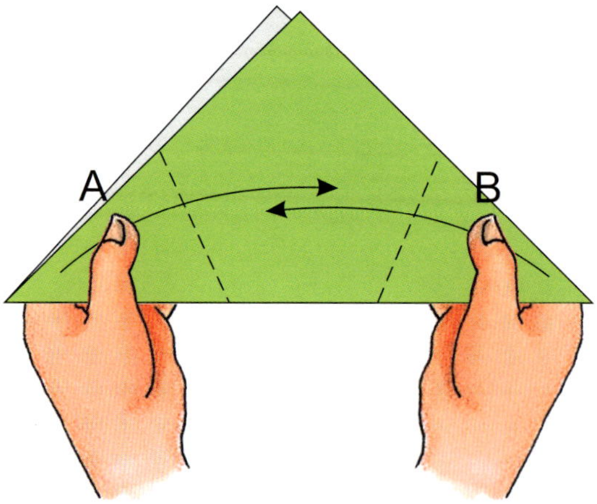

2 Fold the left corner to the right side touching point ‘B’ and fold the right corner to the left side touching point ‘A’.

3 Fold the upper layer of the triangle in half along the dotted line.

4 Fold this flap in half again along the dotted line.

5 Fold once more and crease firmly as shown.

6 Finished.

Whale

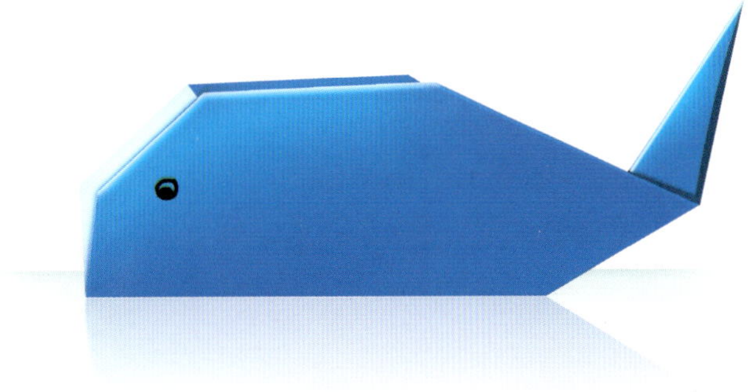

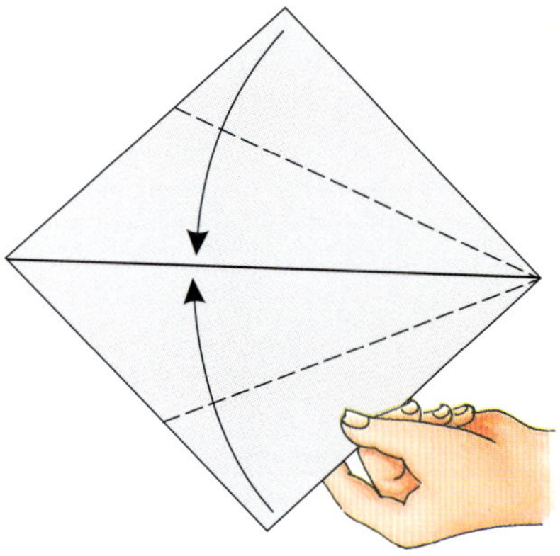

1 Make a centre crease and unfold it. Fold the top and bottom corners to the centre line.

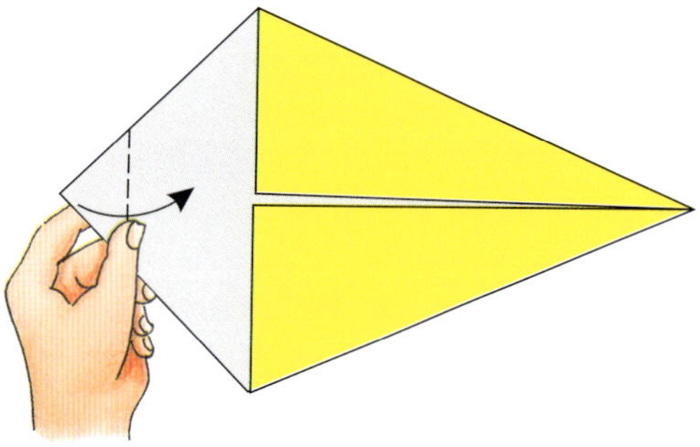

2 Fold the left tip inside along the dotted line.

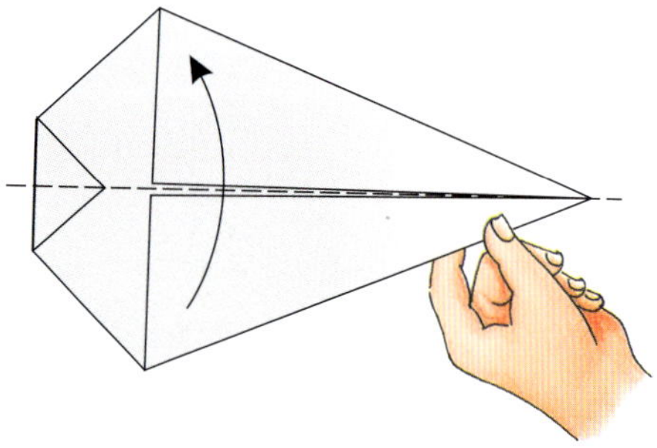

3 Now fold in half along the dotted line.

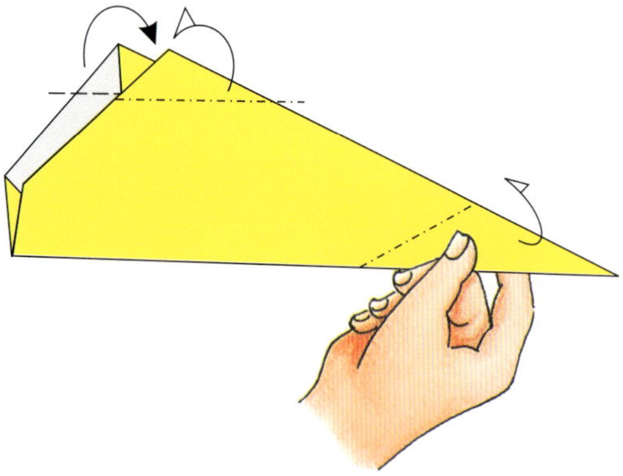

4 Fold both the upper tips inside. Fold the right tip backwards to make the tail.

5 Draw eyes and mouth and the whale is ready.

Collage Work

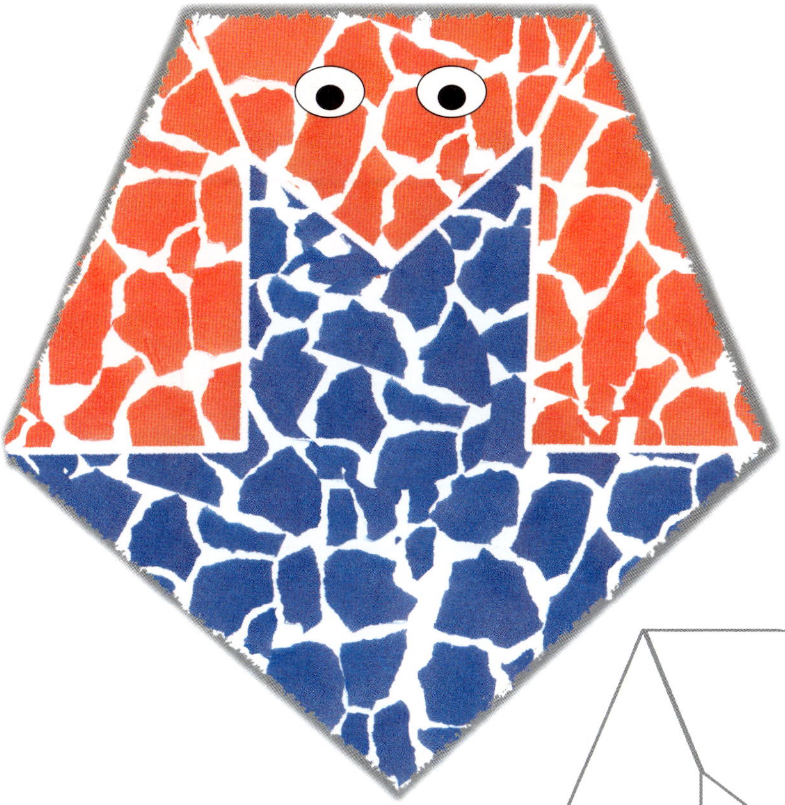

Owl

TIPS AND TRICKS

Step-1 Collect paper sheets of various colours of your own choice. Tear them in small pieces of different shapes.

Step-2 Set them within the outline and paste in the given shape.

Cut and Paste

Crown

TIPS AND TRICKS

Step-1 Take craft paper sheets of various colours. Trace different parts on the shape of different colours.

Step-2 Now paste these pieces at the appropriate places.

Crushed Paper Art

Santa's Cap

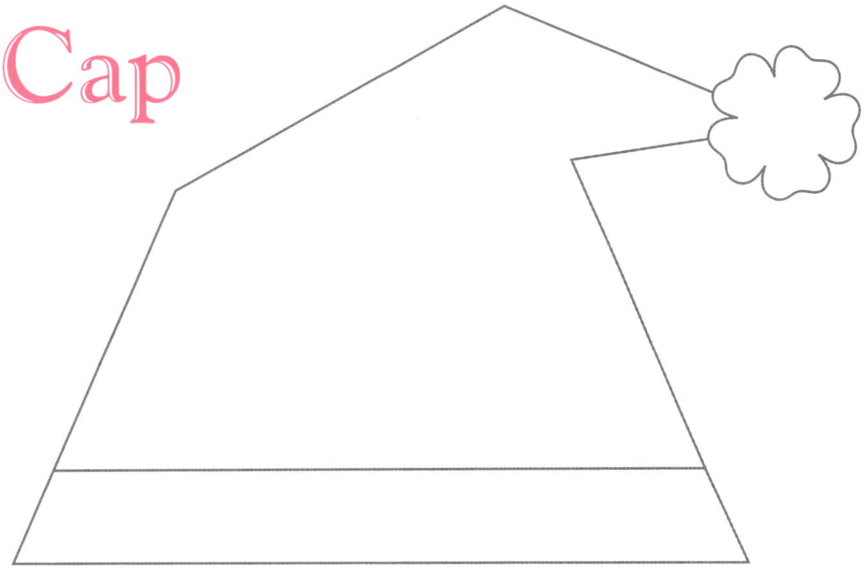

TIPS AND TRICKS

Step-1 Take a plain paper and squeeze it in your hand. Open it gently and apply the poster colour with a flat brush.

Step-2 Now cut the paper according to the shape and paste it within the outline.

Spray Paint

Whale

TIPS AND TRICKS

Step-1 Take a white paper. Spray different colours of your own choice with a tooth brush on the white paper.

Step-2 Cut the parts of the shape as per your liking and paste them on the figure.

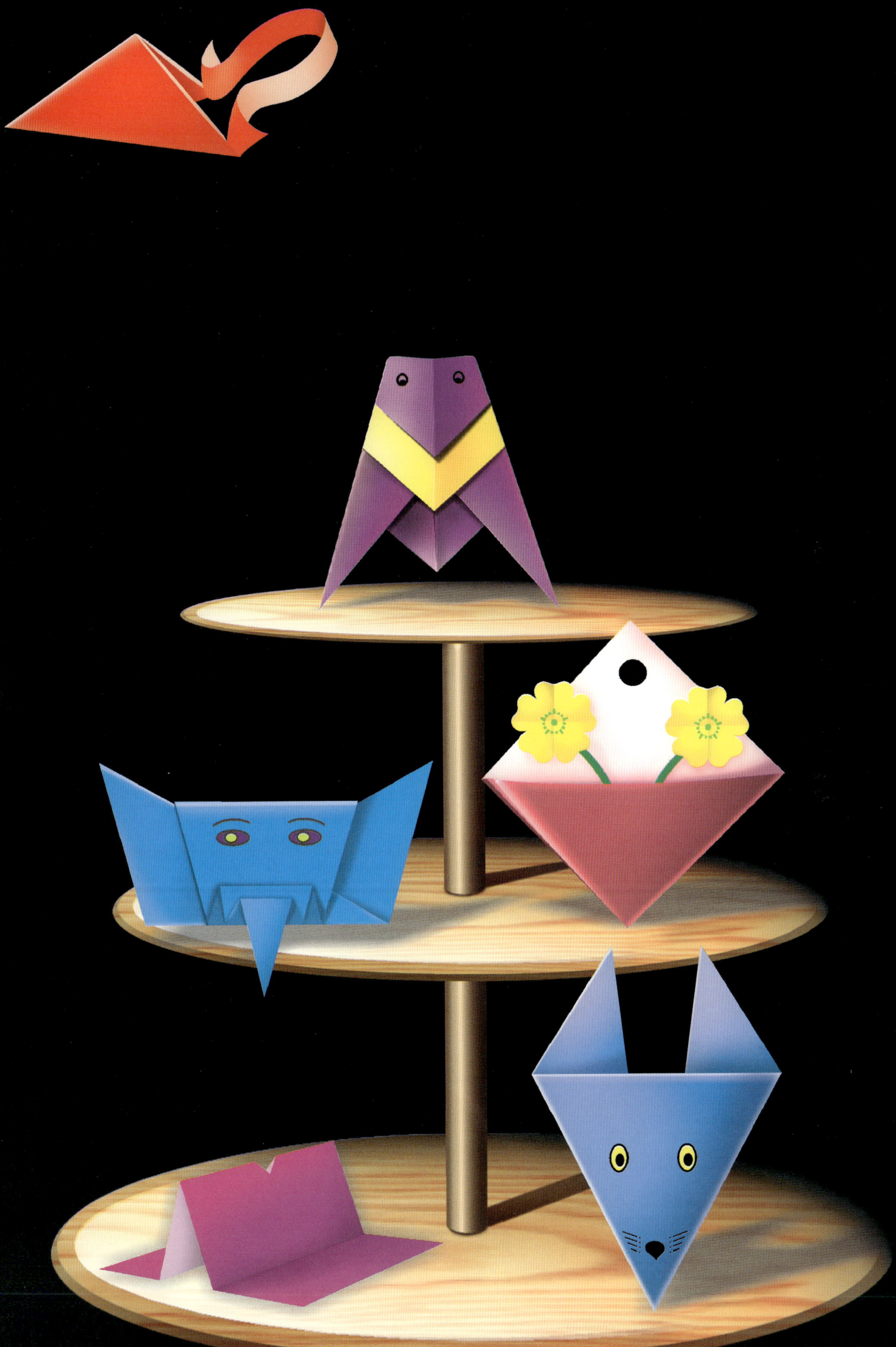

Whistle

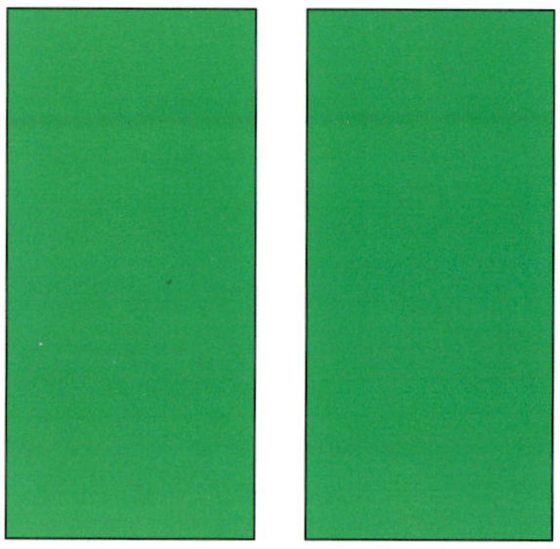

1 Use half of the paper.

2 Fold along the dotted line.

3 Fold the upper sheet upward to meet the other end.

4 Fold the other side backwards in the same way.

5 Use a scissors to cut the upper edge as shown.

6 Your whistle is ready to blow.

Fox Head

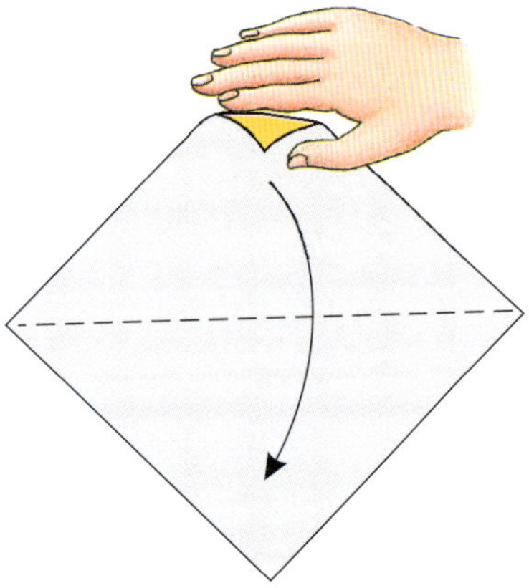

1 Fold along the dotted line in direction of arrow.

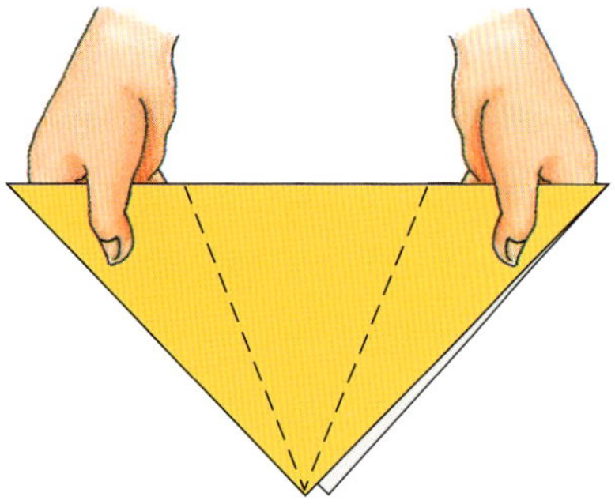

2 Fold the right and left corners upwards along the dotted lines....

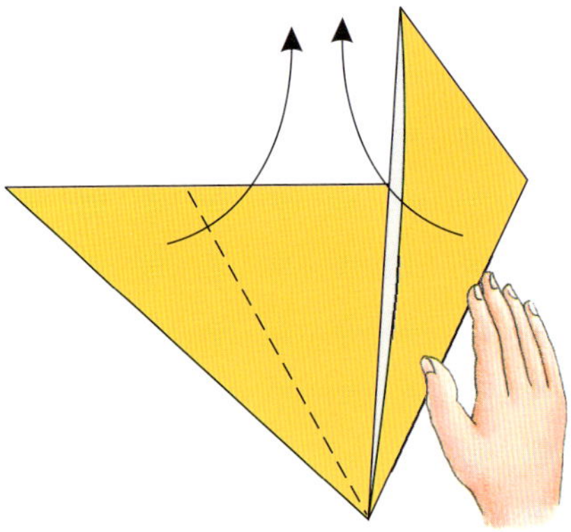

3 .... like this.

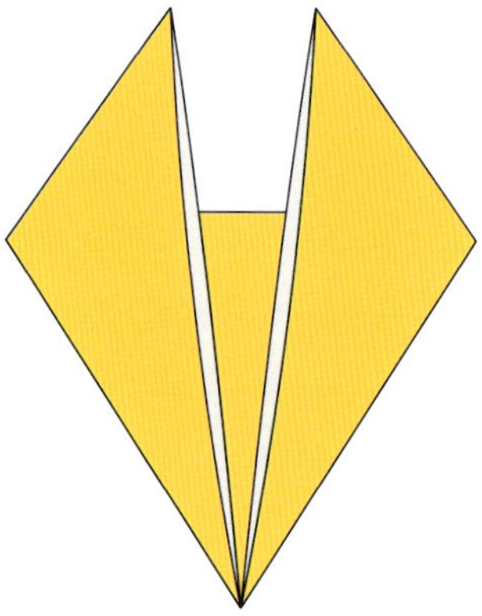

4 It will form the fox's raised ears.

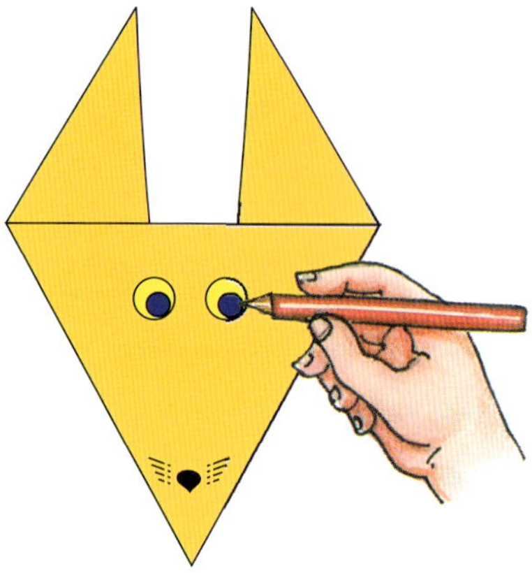

5 Draw the eyes and nose, and your fox head is ready.

Elephant Cap

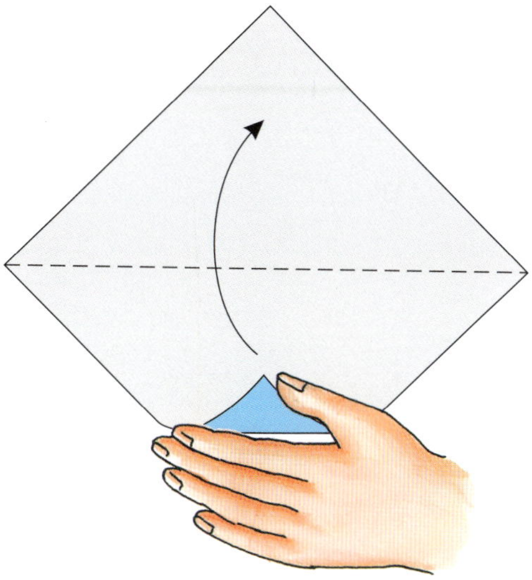

1 Make a fold along the dotted line in the direction of arrow.

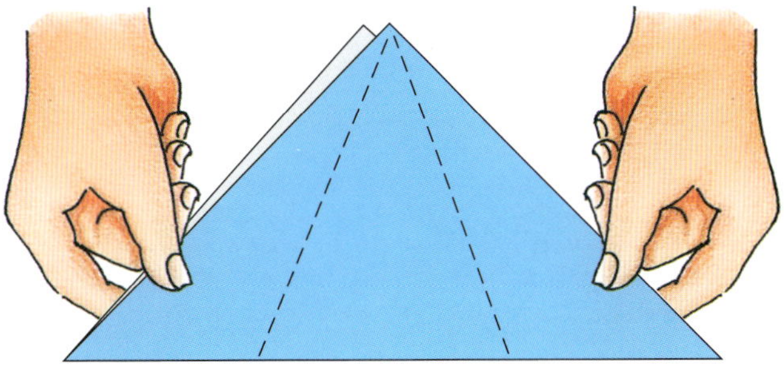

2 Draw two lines to divide the paper into three equal parts.

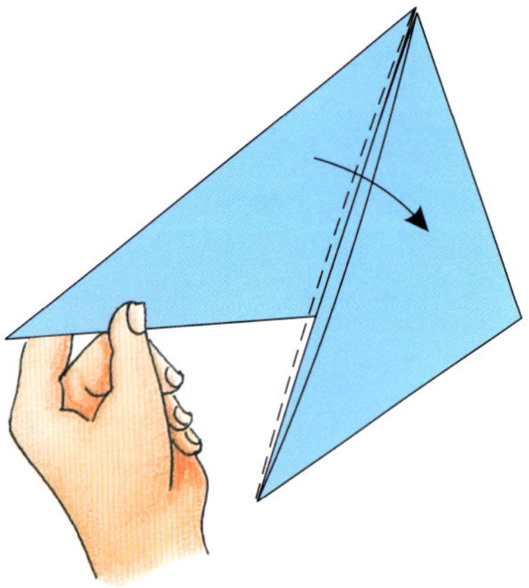

3 Fold the right flap and then fold the left flap along the dotted line to overlap the right flap as shown.

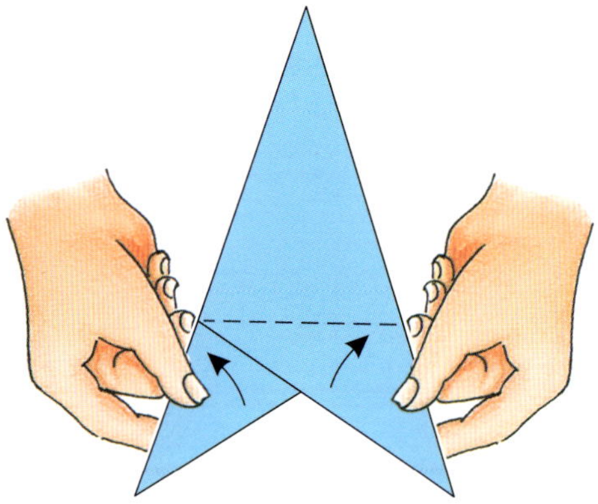

4 Fold both the corners upward along the dotted line.

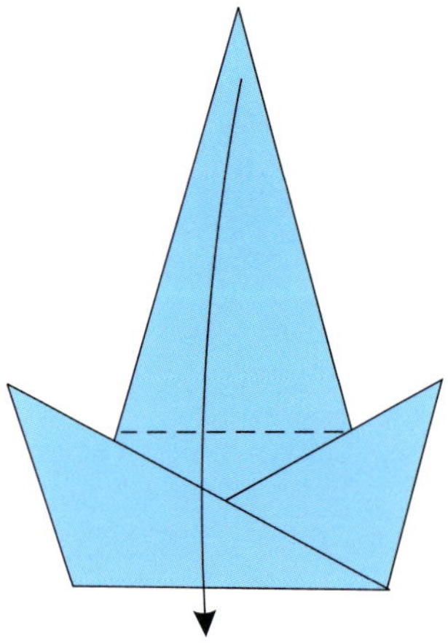

5 Fold the upper tip downwards along the dotted line.

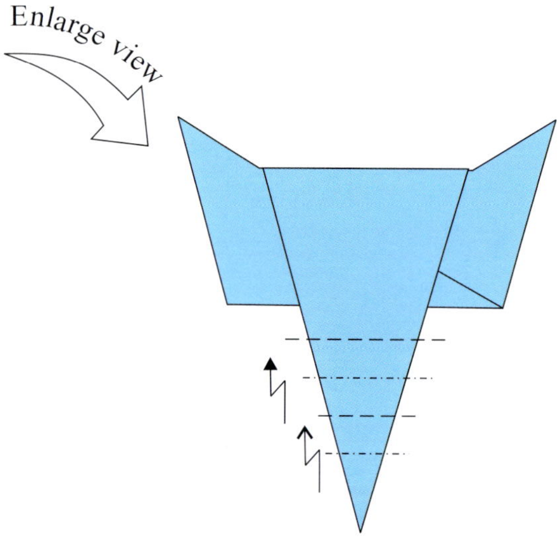

6 For making an elephant cap, fold the drooping flap forward and backward alternately to form the trunk.

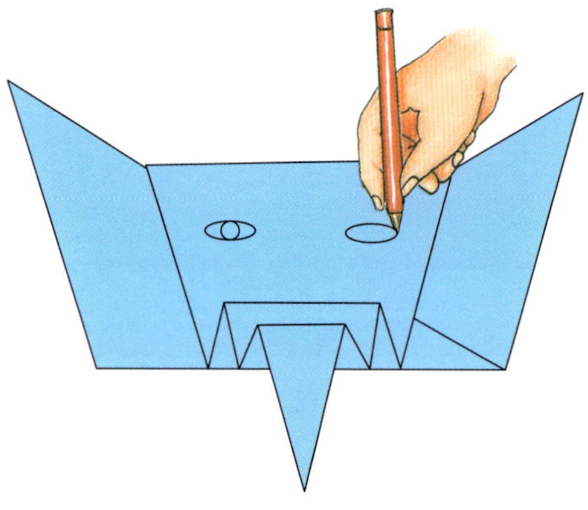

7 Draw eyes like this. The elephant cap is ready.

Flower Basket

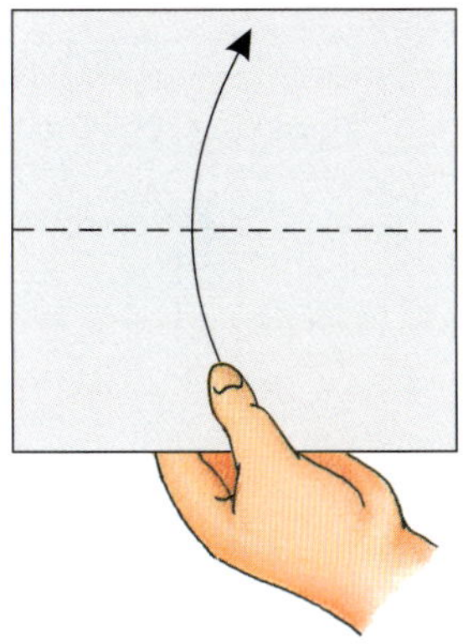

1 Fold the paper in half along the dotted line.

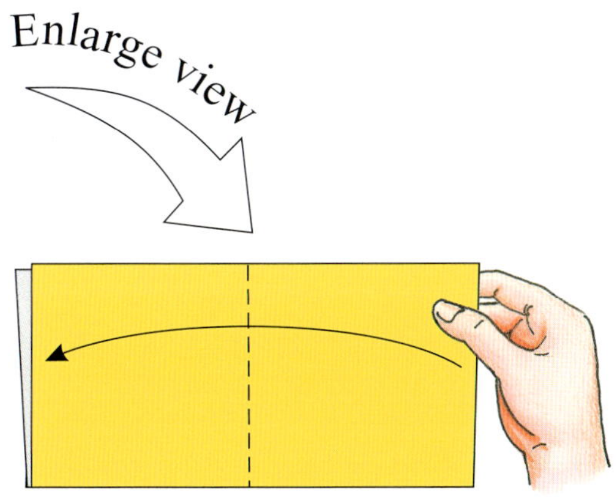

2 Fold it in half again from right to left.

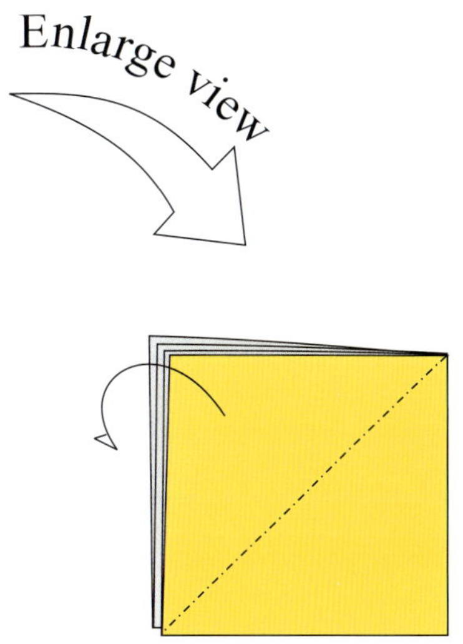

3 Fold all the four flaps backwards. Crease them firmly and then open.

4 Neatly, push the first three flaps inside to form a pocket. Your flower basket is ready.

5 Punch a hole at the top and hang it on a wall with some paper flowers in it.

Housefly

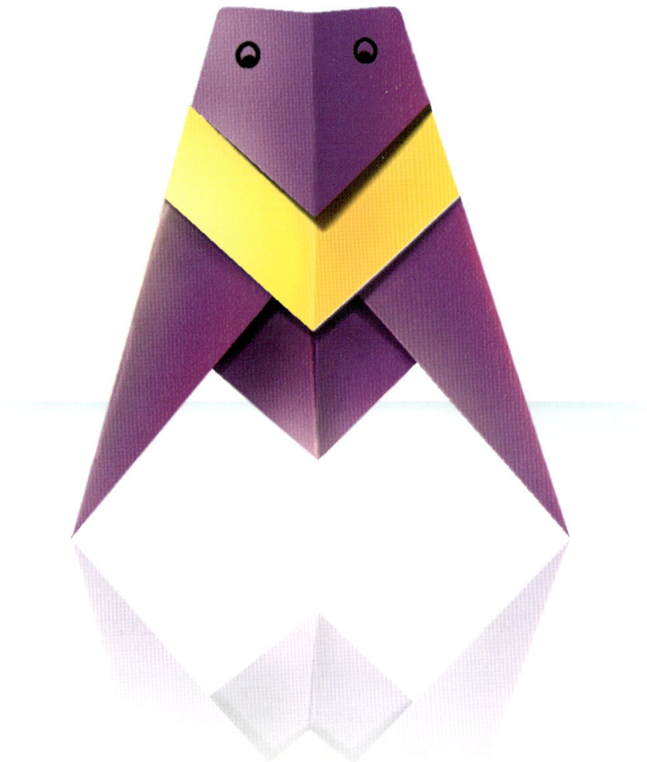

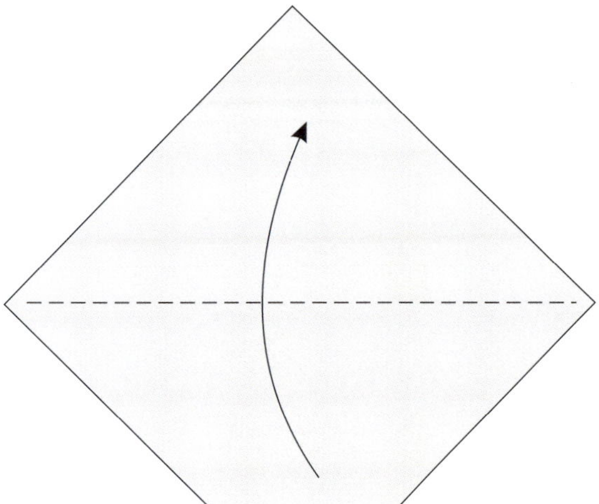

1 Fold in half along the dotted line.

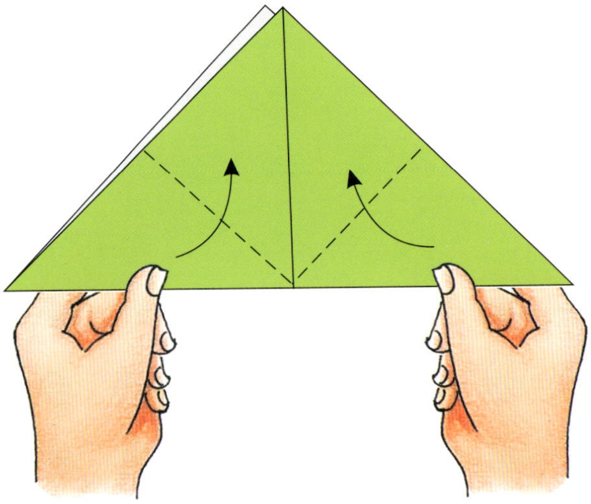

2 Fold both the side corners to the centre along the dotted lines.

3 Fold both the upper flaps downwards along the dotted line.

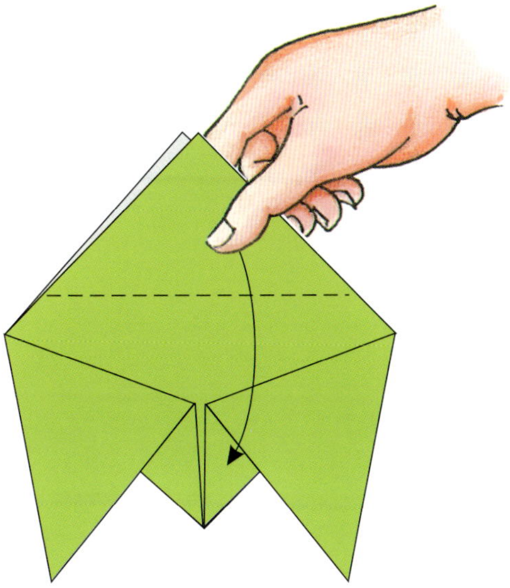

4 Fold the top front layer downwards along the dotted line as shown.

5 Fold the back flap downwards to overlap the first.

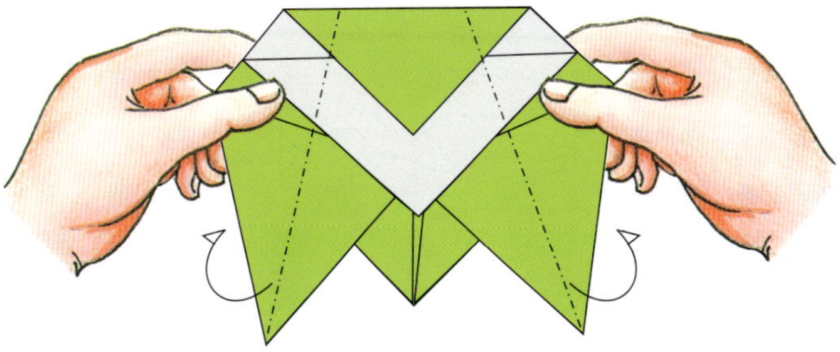

6 Fold both the sides backwards as shown.

7 Draw two big eyes and your housefly model is ready!

Sun Cap

1 Take a paper of size 8" x 12" or you may take a centre page from your rough note-book.

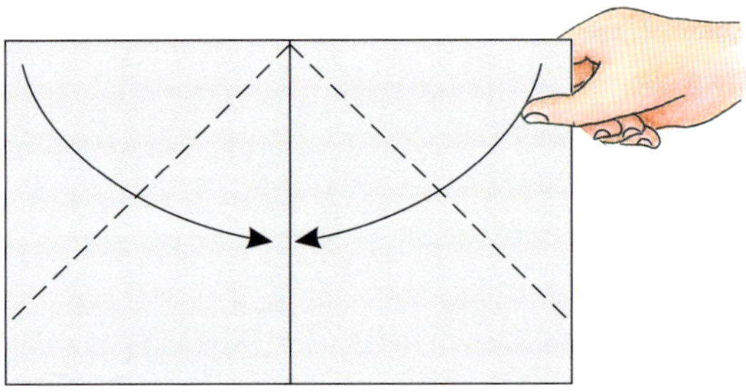

2 Fold the top left and right corners to meet the centre line.

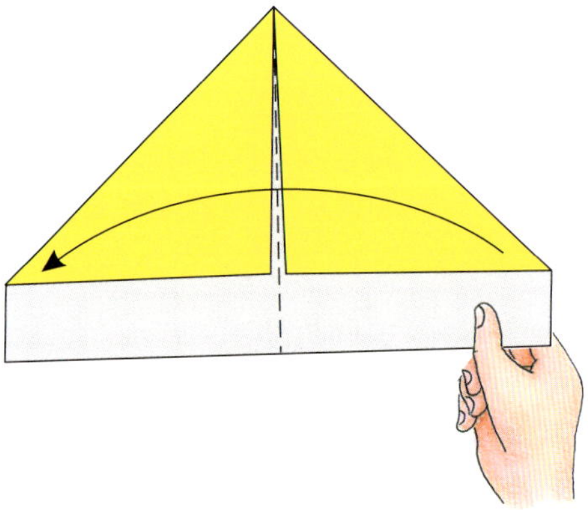

3 Fold in half along the dotted line.

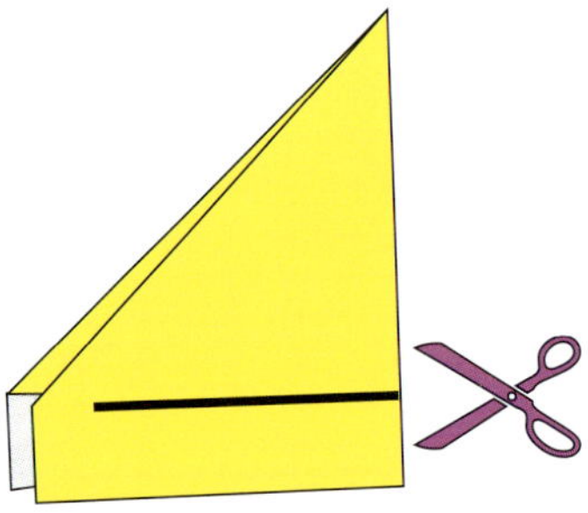

4 Make a cut along the lower edge of the triangles.

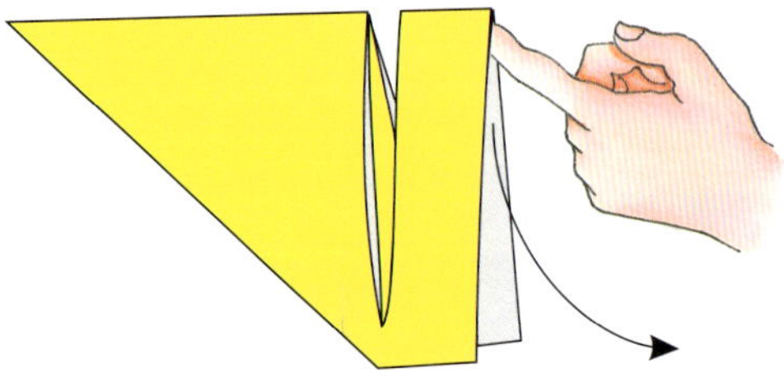

5 Pull the flap gently and wear your sun cap.

Collage Work

Fox Head

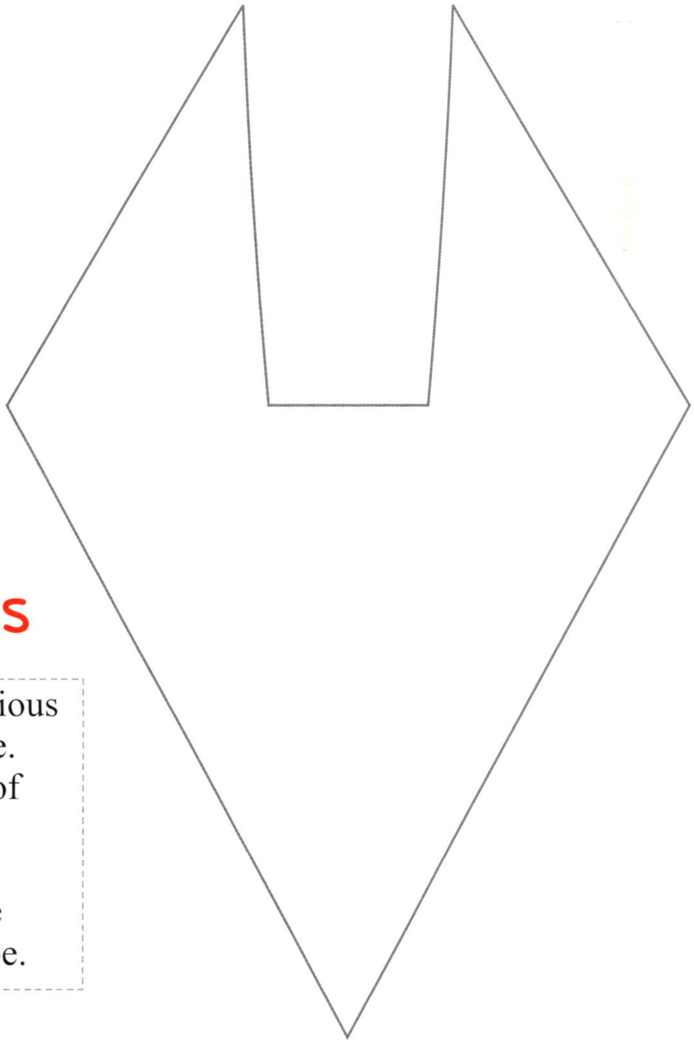

TIPS AND TRICKS

Step-1 Collect paper sheets of various colours of your own choice. Tear them in small pieces of different shapes.

Step-2 Set them within the outline and paste in the given shape.

Cut and Paste

Flower Basket

TIPS AND TRICKS

Step-1 Take craft paper sheets of various colours. Trace different parts on the shape of different colours.

Step-2 Now paste these pieces at the appropriate places.

Crushed Paper Art

House Fly

TIPS AND TRICKS

Step-1 Take a plain paper and squeeze it in your hand. Open it gently and apply the poster colour with a flat brush.

Step-2 Now cut the paper according to the shape and paste it within the outline.

Spray Paint

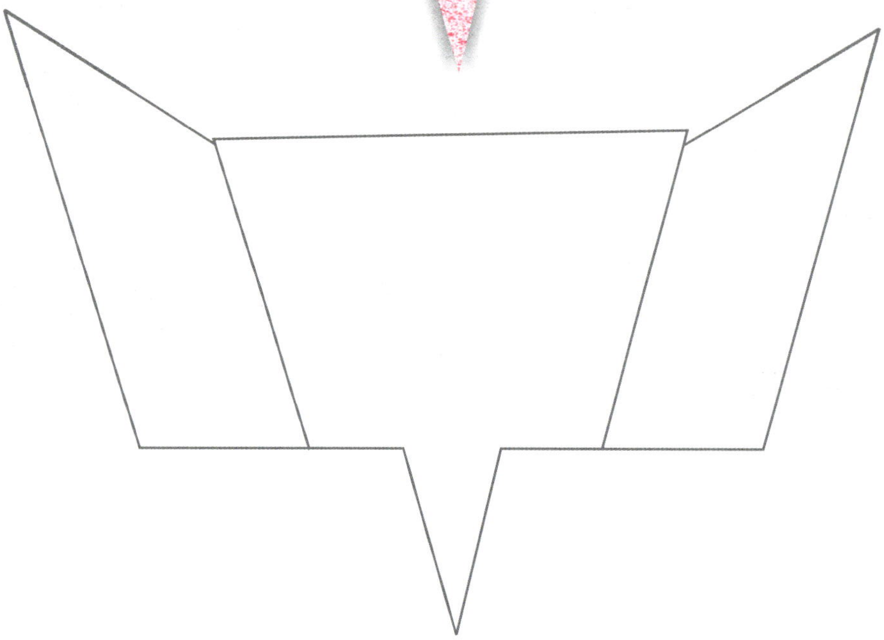

Elephant Cap

TIPS AND TRICKS

Step-1 Take a white paper. Spray different colours of your own choice with a tooth brush on the white paper.

Step-2 Cut the parts of the shape as per your liking and paste them on the figure.

Joker's Hat

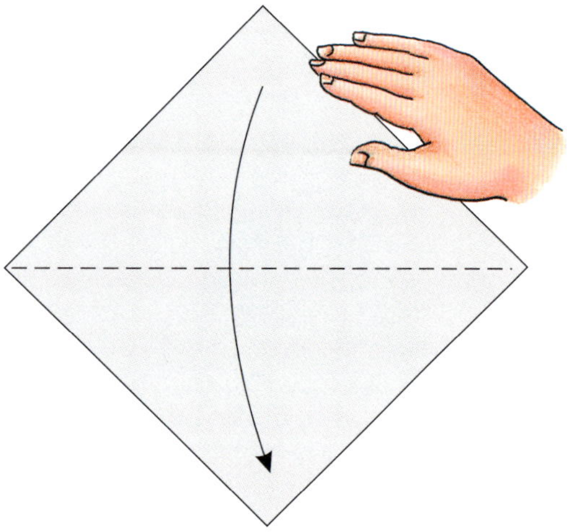

1 Fold the paper in half along the dotted line.

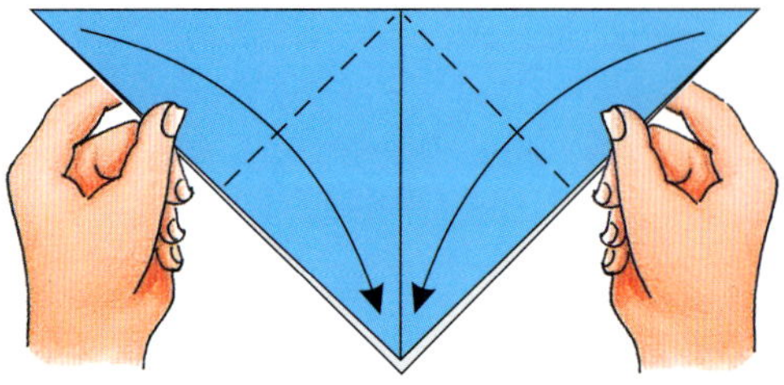

2 Fold the side corners to the centre along the dotted lines.

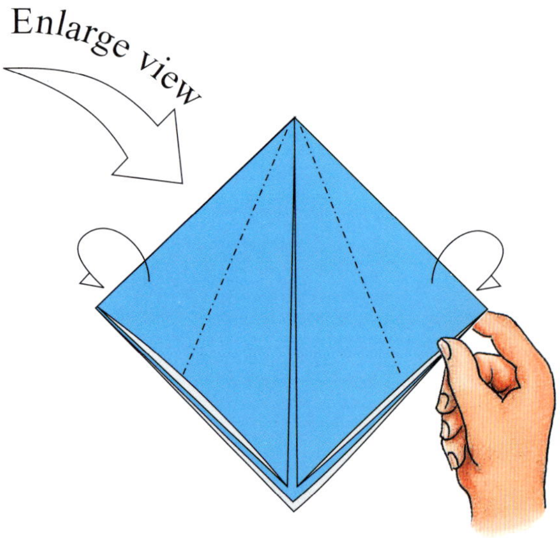

3 Fold the side corners backwards along the dotted lines.

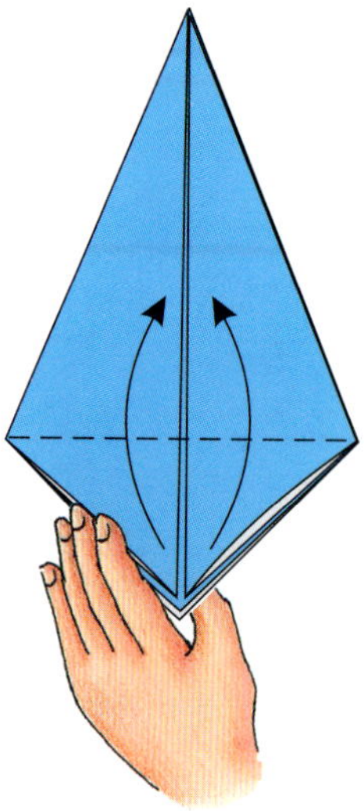

4 Fold both the small triangles upwards along the dotted line.

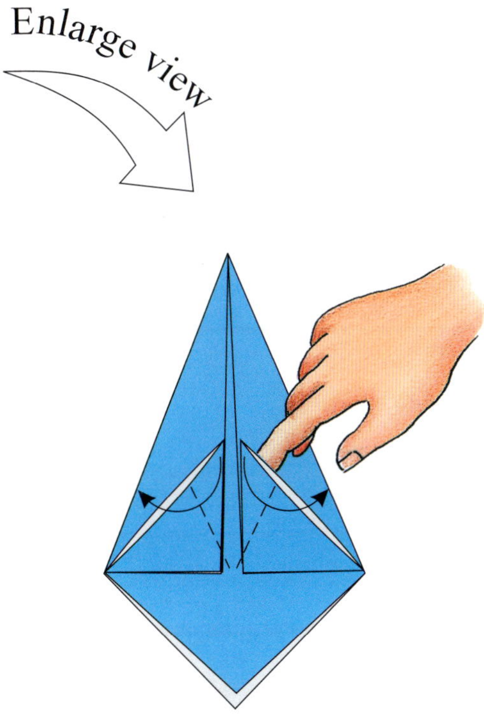

5 Fold the tips outwards along the dotted lines.

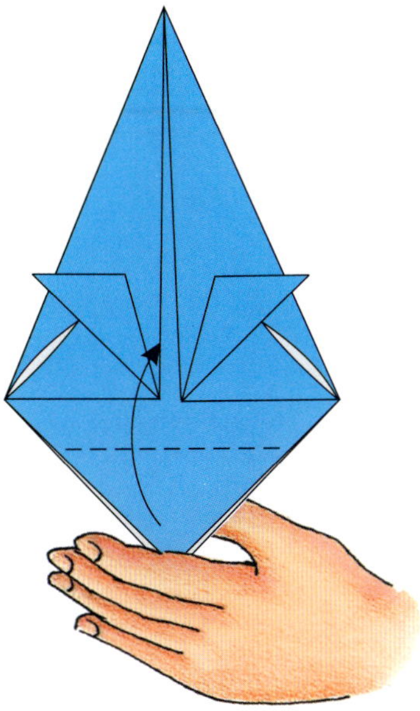

6 Fold only the upper layer of the bottom flap.

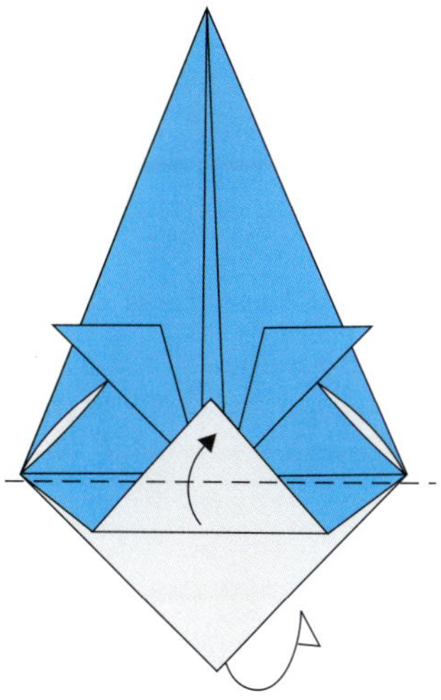

7 Fold the front flap upwards. Now fold the lower flap backwards as shown.

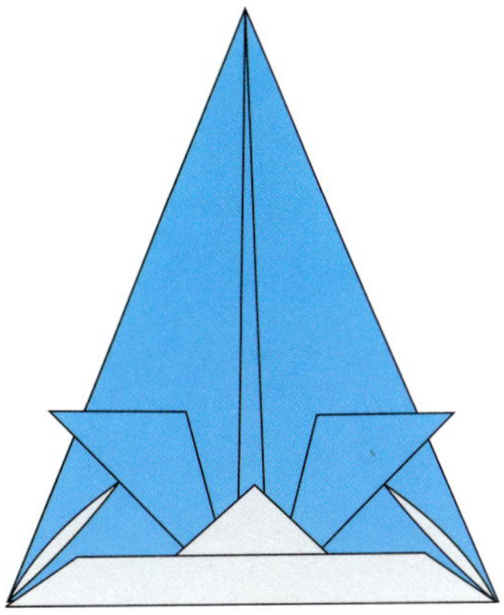

8 Your joker's hat is ready.

Pop-up Greeting Card

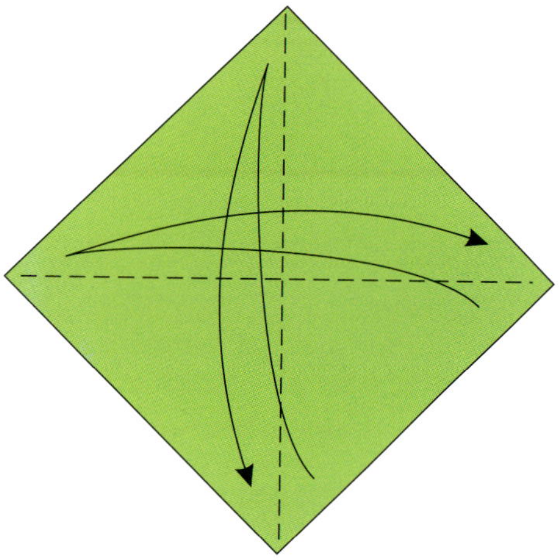

1 Fold the paper in half along each diagonal to make a centre crease and unfold it.

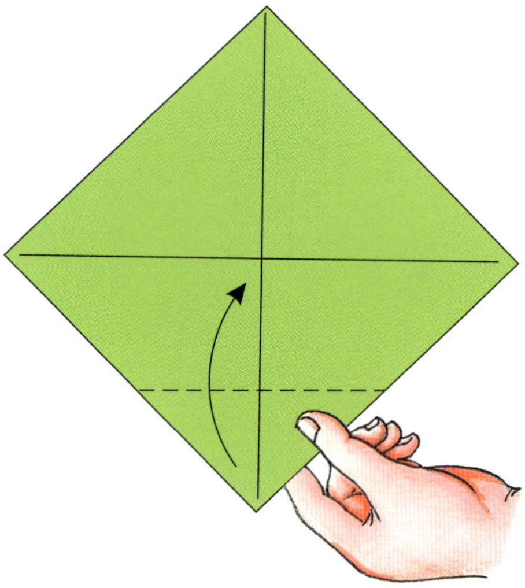

2 Fold the lower corner to the centre along the dotted line.

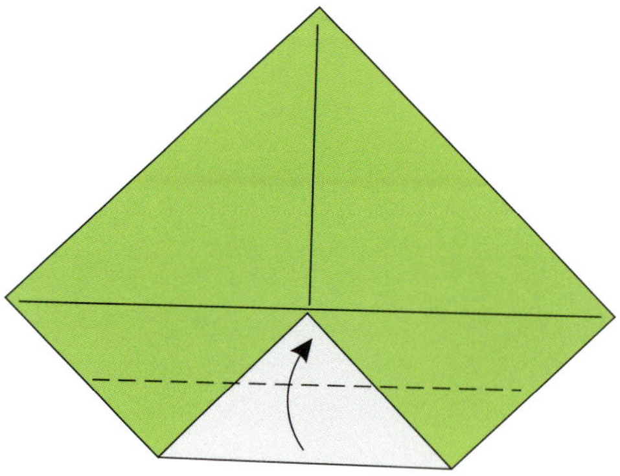

3 Fold the bottom edge to the centre line....

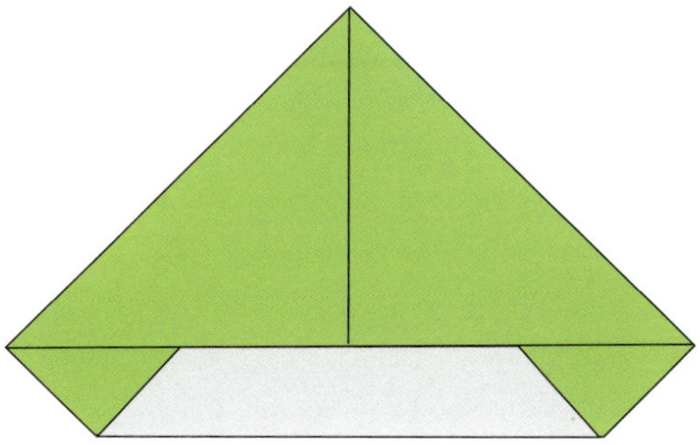

4 .... like this and unfold.

5 Cut along the crease.

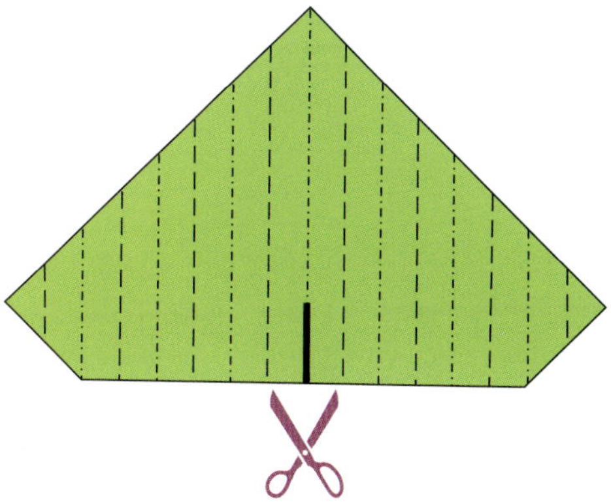

6 Make a small cut in the middle and fold the model forward and backward alternately.

7 Decorate it and pull out the bottom halves along the cut. Paste them at the centre of a greeting card.

Shirt

1 Use half sheet of a paper.

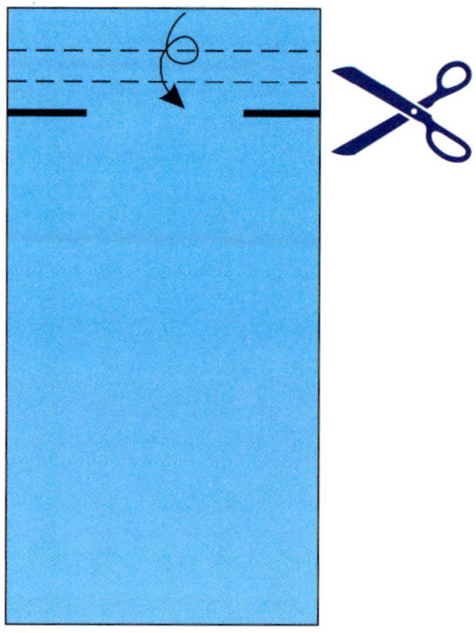

2 Fold the upper flap twice along the dotted lines and make cuts as shown.

3 Fold along the dotted lines in the direction of arrows.

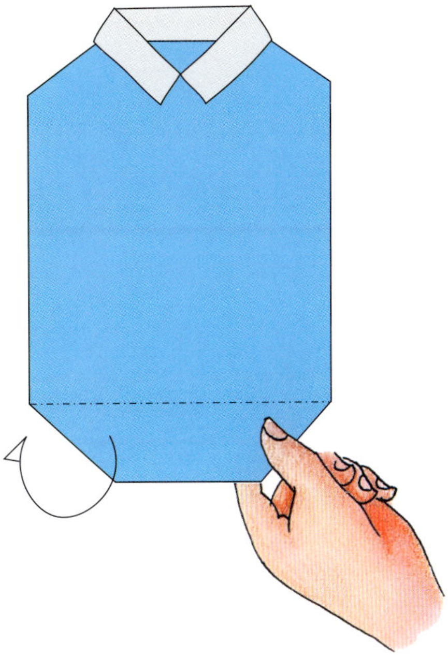

5 Fold the bottom edge backward along the dotted line.

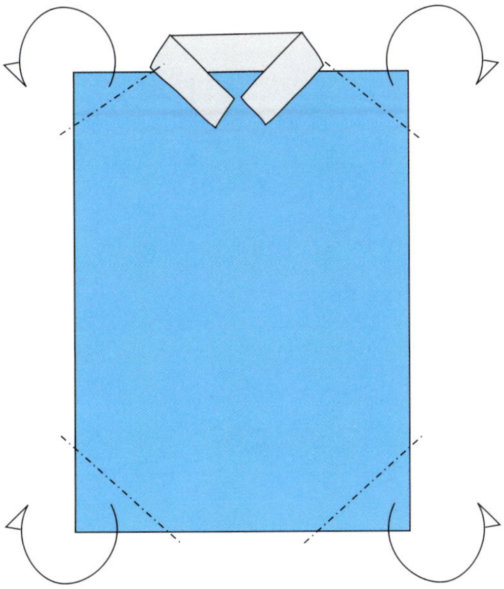

4 Fold all the four corners backward.

6 Draw line and buttons. Now, your shirt is ready.

Star

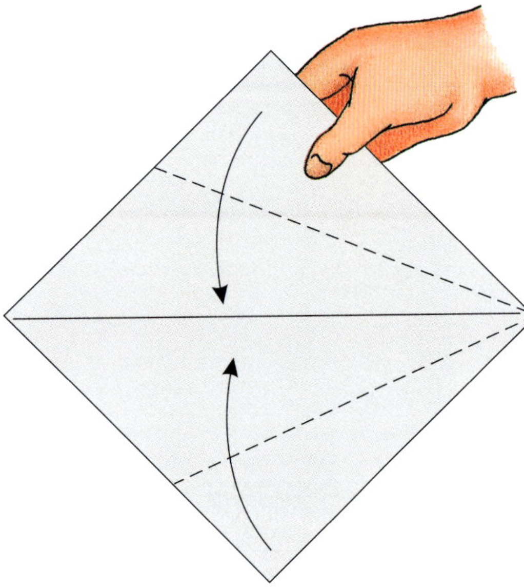

1 Fold the top and bottom corners to the centre line.

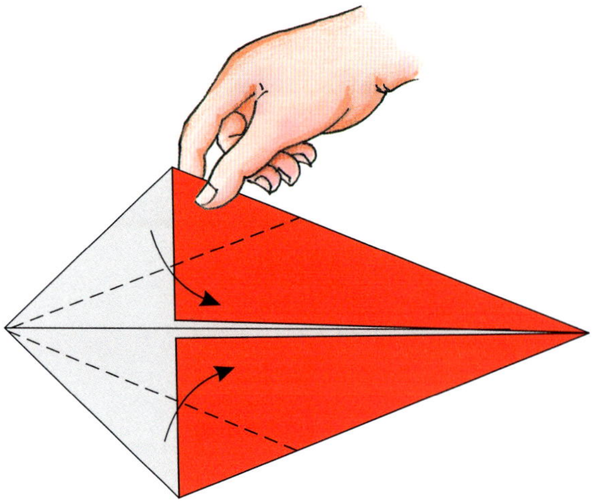

2 Again fold the corners to the centre along the dotted lines.

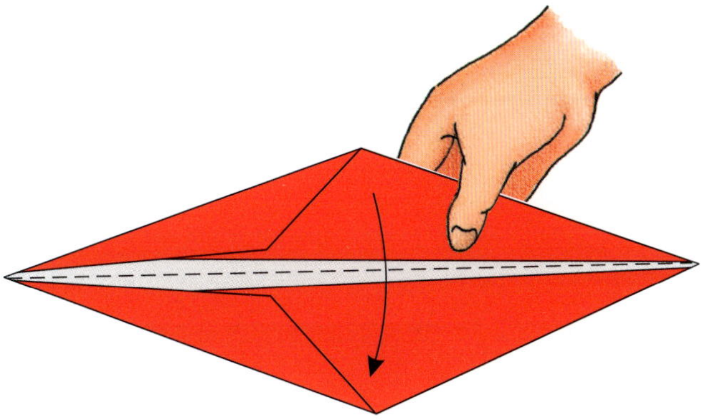

3 Fold in half in the direction of arrow.

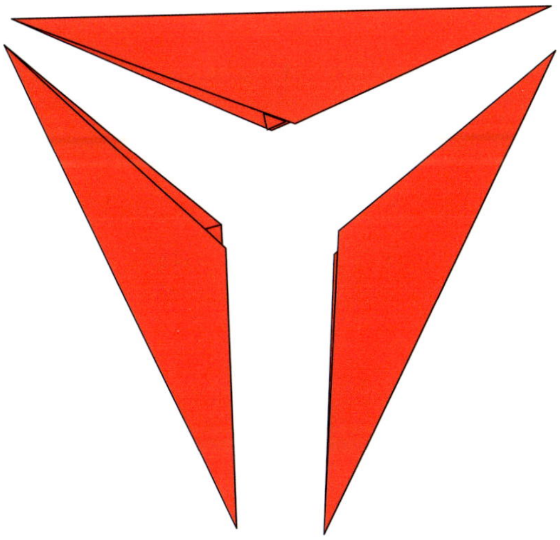

4 Similarly, make two more triangles.

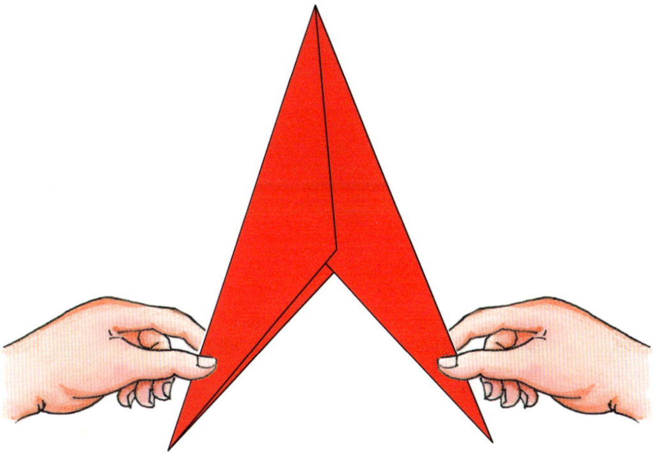

5 Paste two of them together like this.

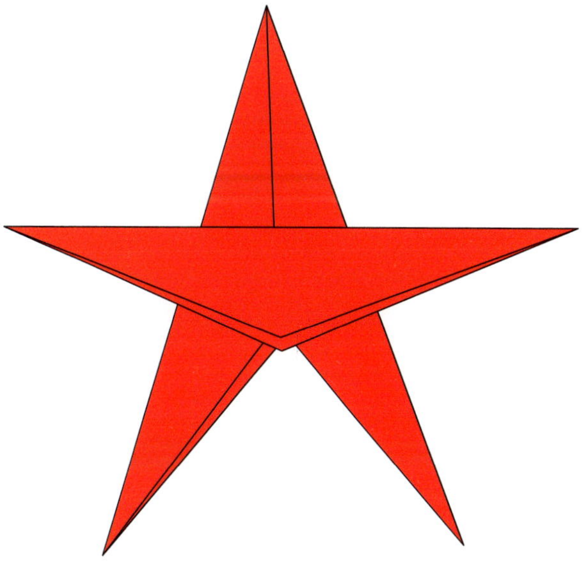

6 Now paste the third triangle as shown, and your star is ready.

Bird

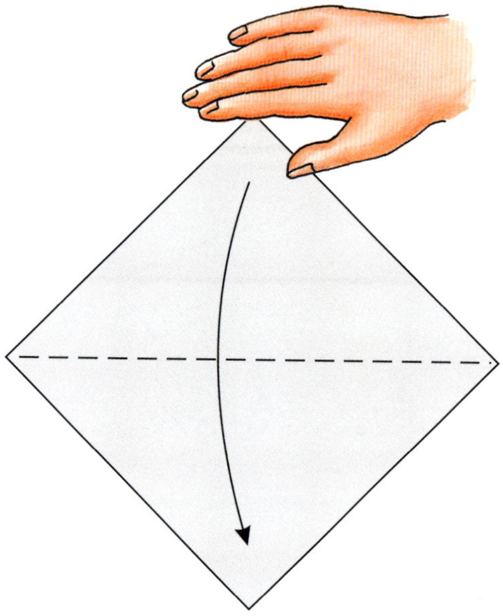

1 Fold in half along the dotted line.

2 Fold and then unfold to make a crease in the middle.

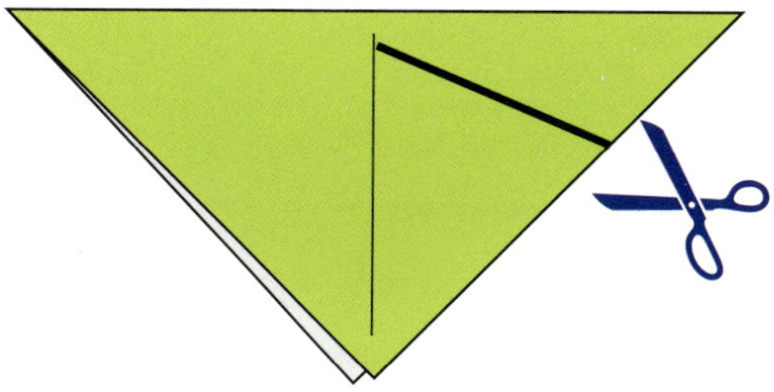

3 Make a cut up to the middle line as shown.

4 Fold the upper and lower layers upwards from the dotted line.

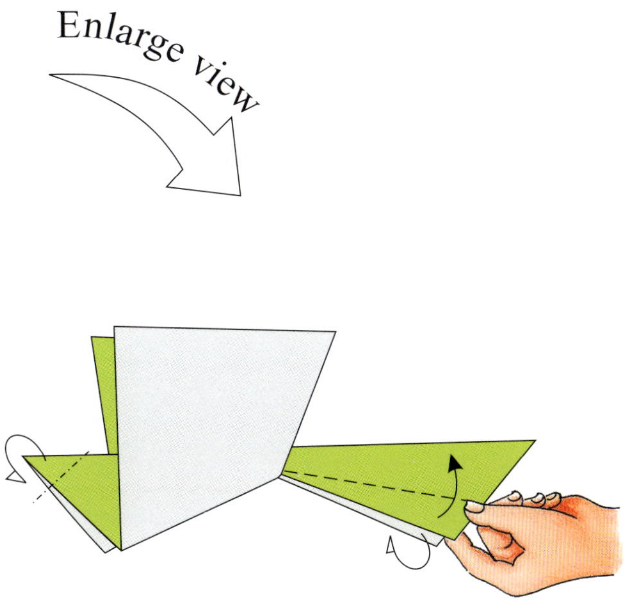

5 Fold the left corner backwards to make the bird's beak.
Fold the right side bottom tips upwards from both sides.

6 Draw an eye, and your bird is ready to fly.

House

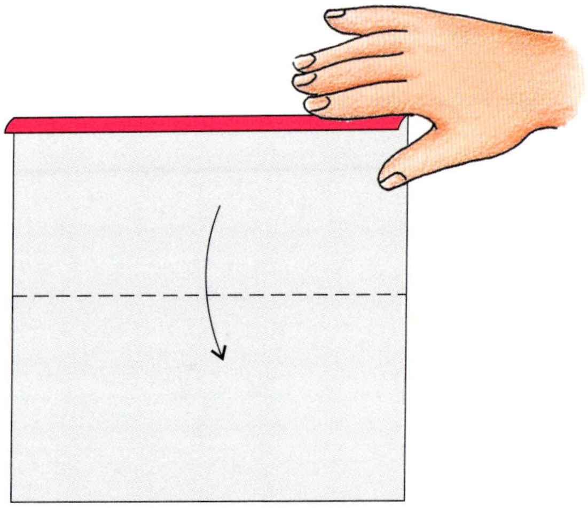

1 Fold in half along the dotted line.

2 Fold in half and unfold to get the centre crease.

3 Fold the right and the left edges to the centre line and unfold.

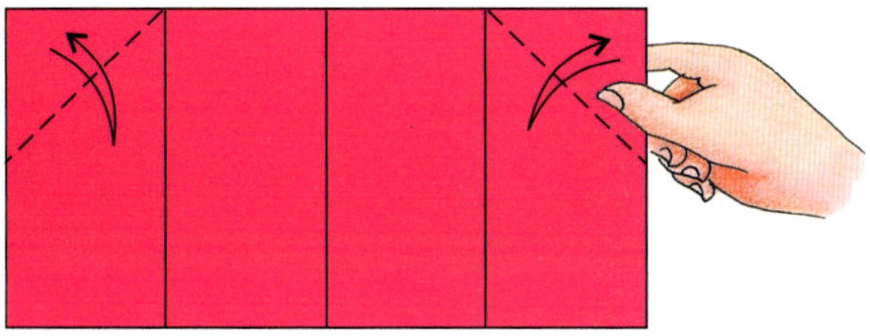

4 Fold the top corners forward and backward and unfold.

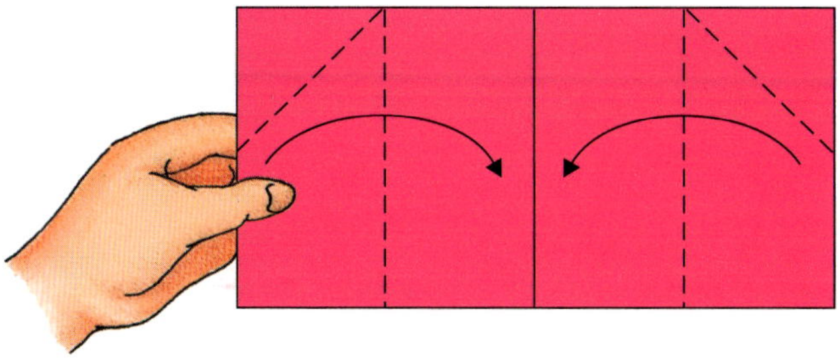

5 Fold inwardly along the dotted lines.

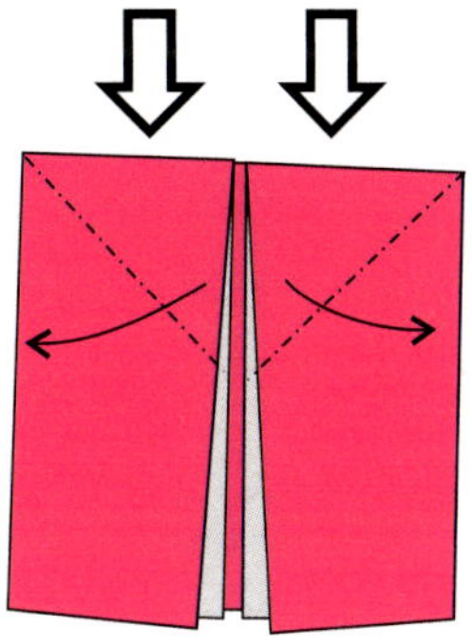

6 Open the upper layers to the left and right as shown.

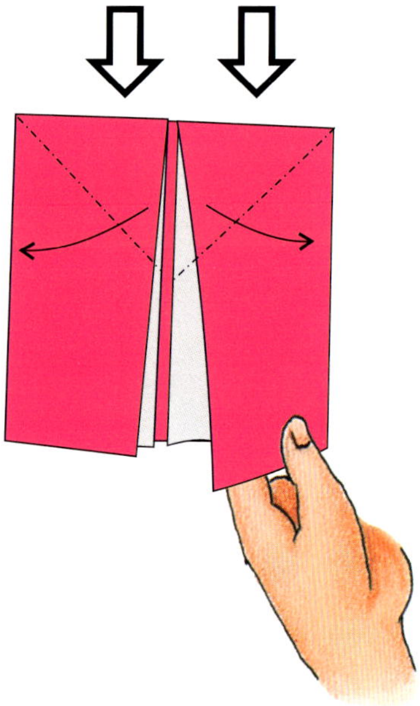

7 It opens out into triangles when flattened.

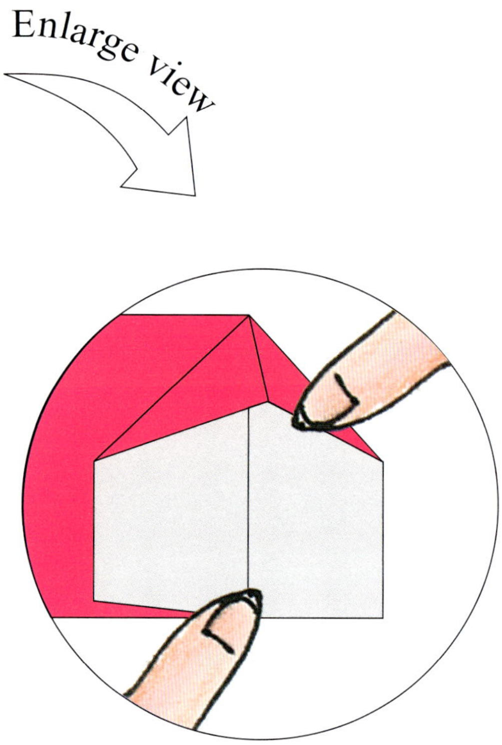

8 Press the upper edges.

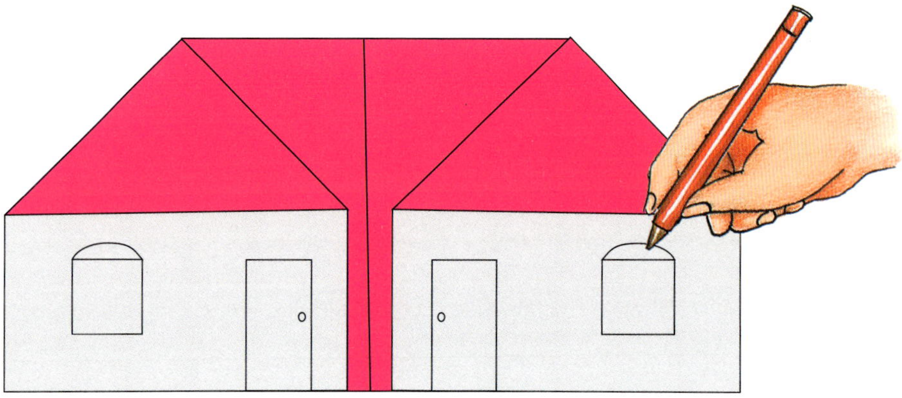

9 Draw windows and doors of the house.

Collage Work

TIPS AND TRICKS

Step-1 Collect paper sheets of various colours of your own choice. Tear them in small pieces of different shapes.

Step-2 Set them within the outline and paste in the given shape.

Joker's hat

Cut and Paste

House

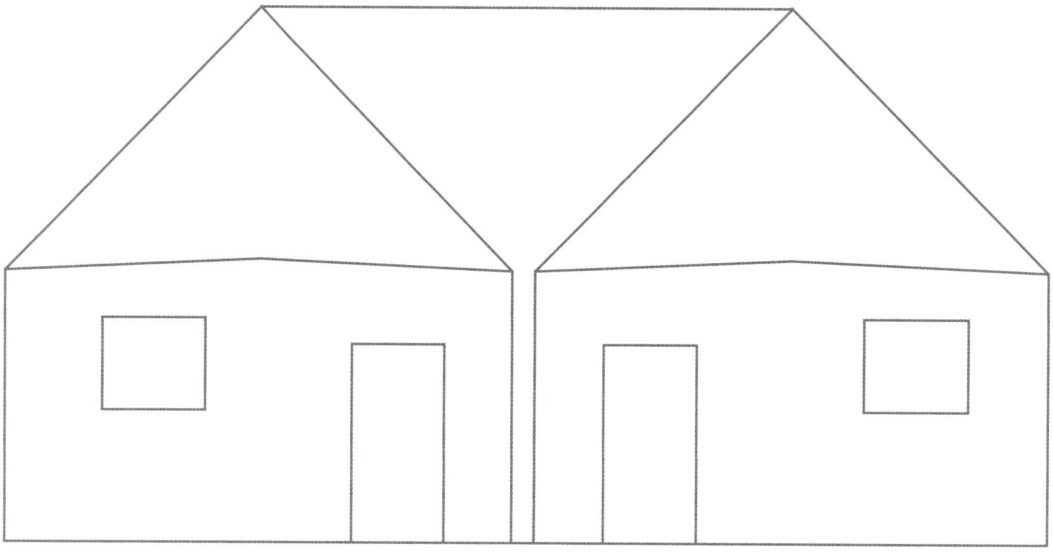

TIPS AND TRICKS

Step-1 Take craft paper sheets of various colours. Trace different parts on the shape of different colours.

Step-2 Now paste these pieces at the appropriate places.

Crushed Paper Art

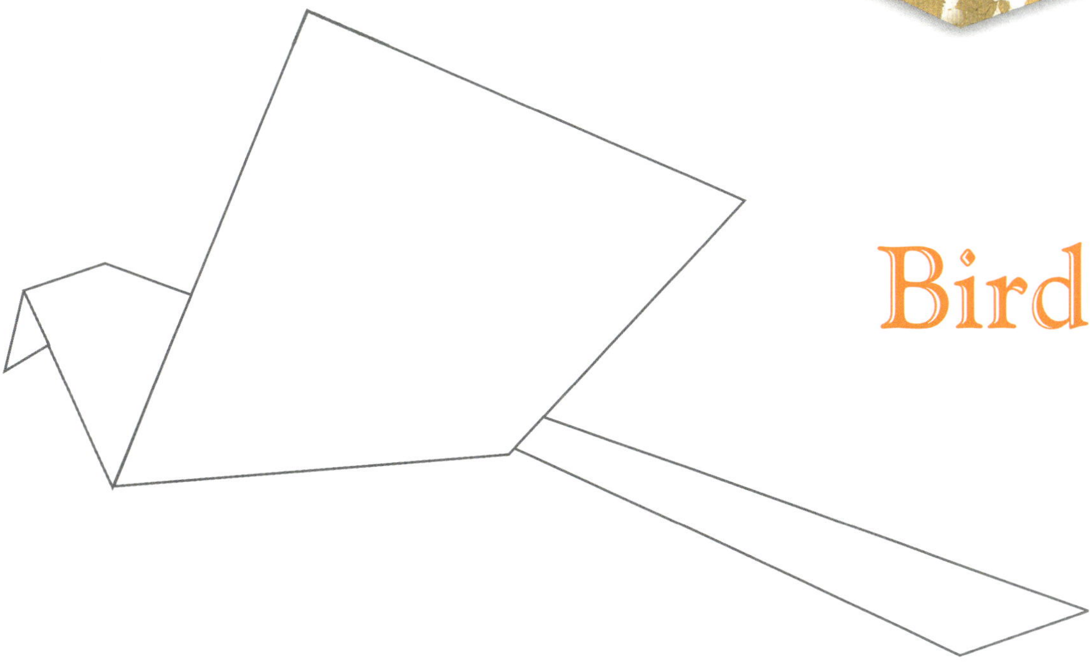

Bird

TIPS AND TRICKS

Step-1 Take a plain paper and squeeze it in your hand. Open it gently and apply the poster colour with a flat brush.

Step-2 Now cut the paper according to the shape and paste it within the outline.

Spray Paint

Pop-up Greeting Card

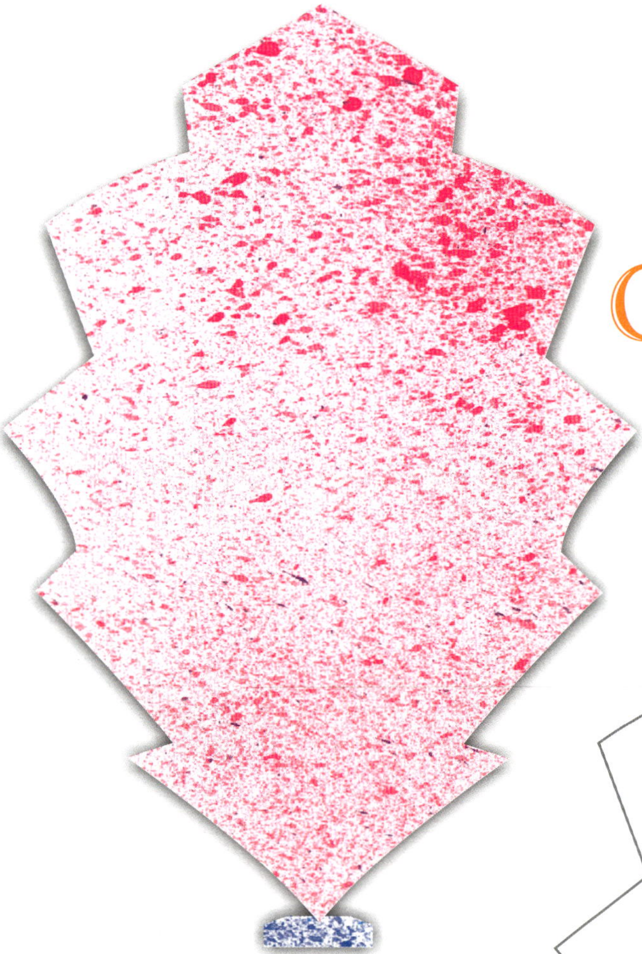

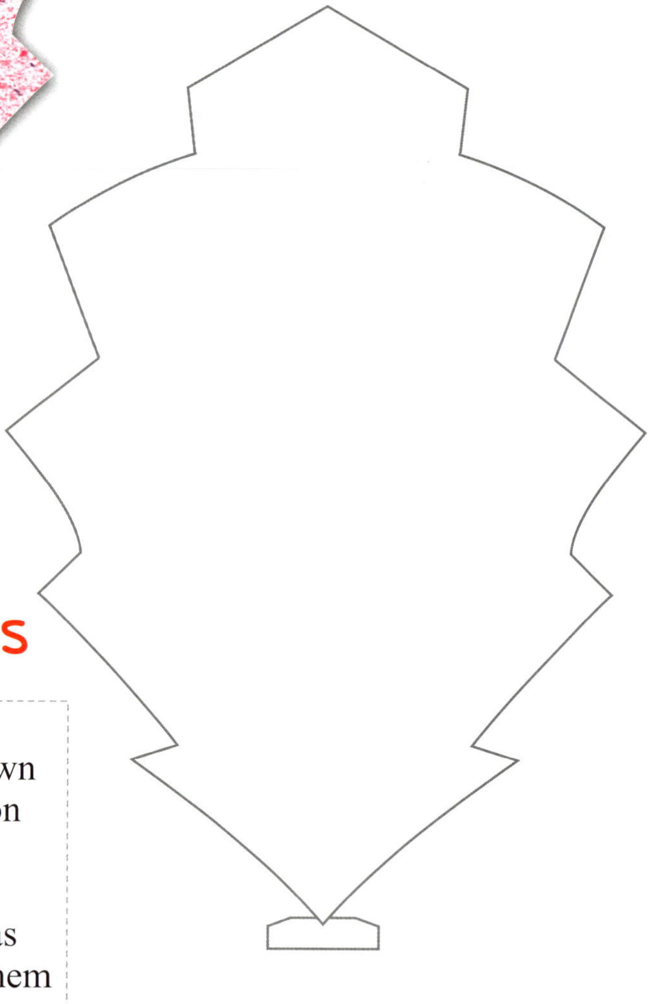

TIPS AND TRICKS

Step-1 Take a white paper. Spray different colours of your own choice with a tooth brush on the white paper.

Step-2 Cut the parts of the shape as per your liking and paste them on the figure.

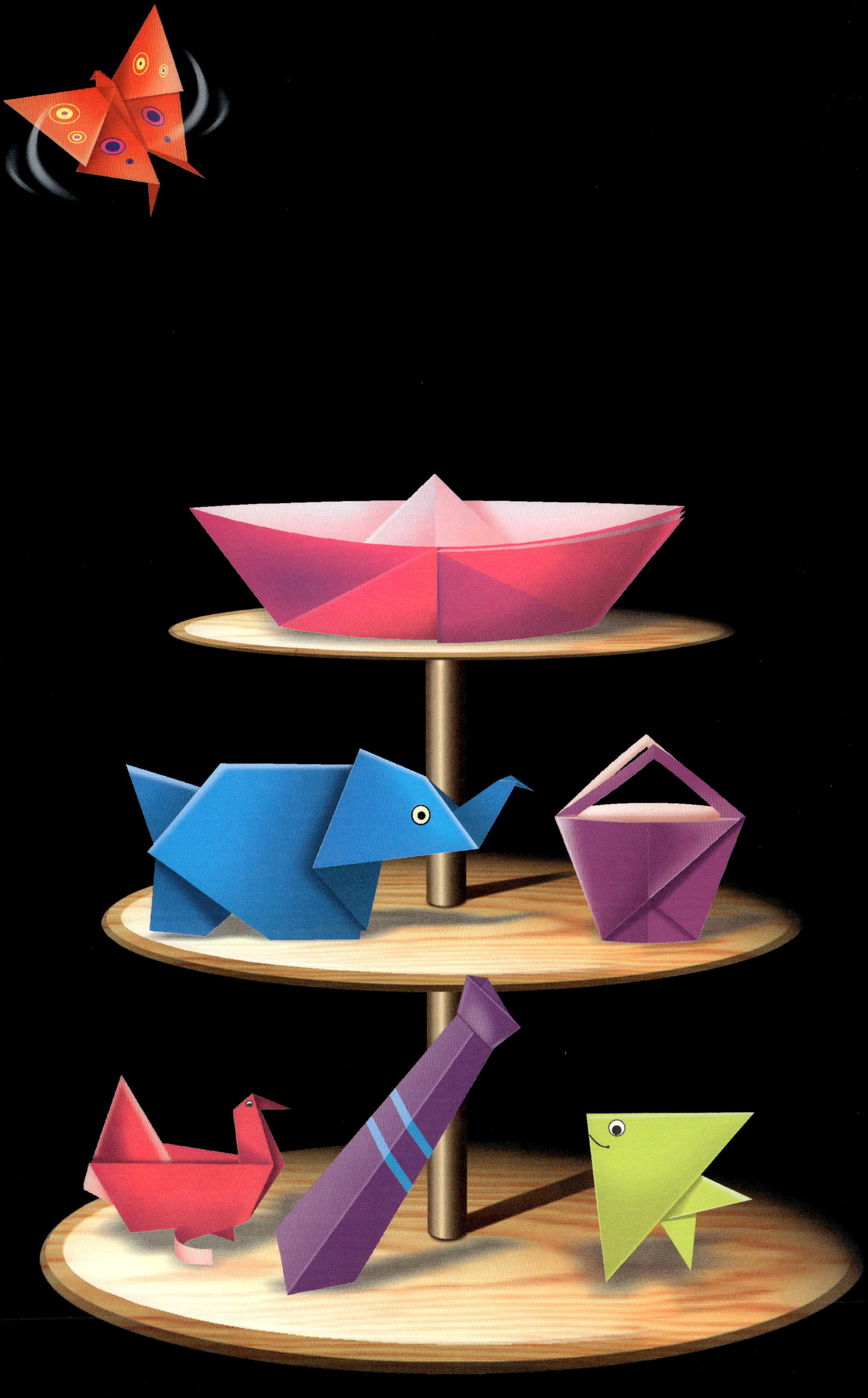

Boat

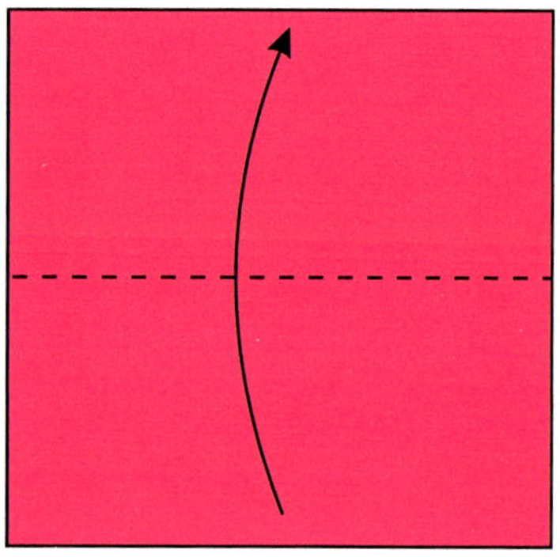

1 Fold in half along the dotted line.

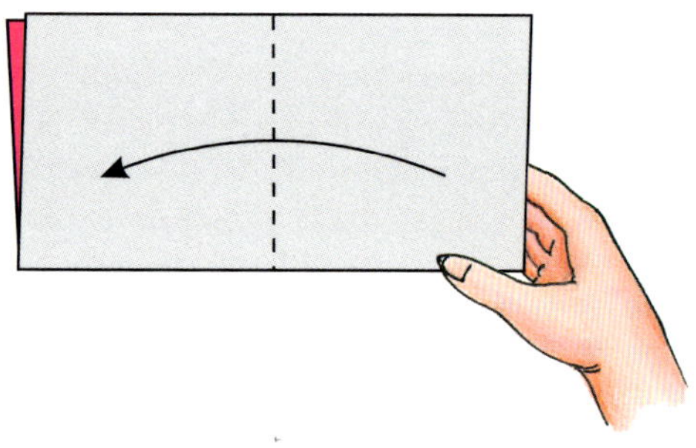

2 Fold in half again along the dotted line.

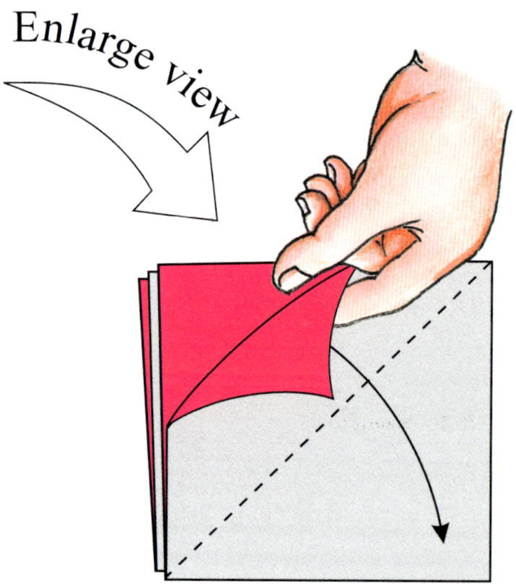

3 Fold the upper layer downward.

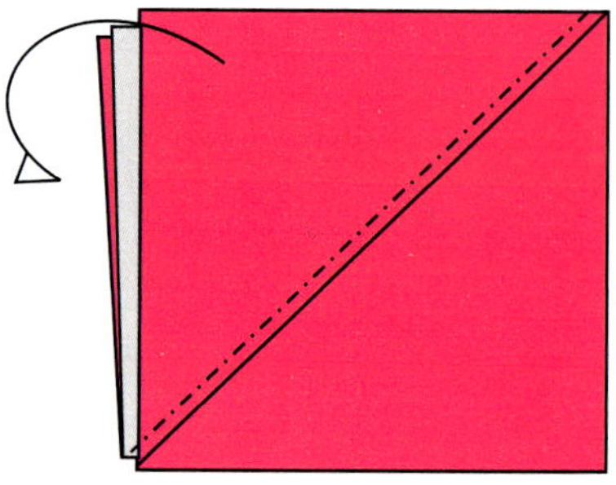

4 Fold the other three flaps backwards and crease firmly....

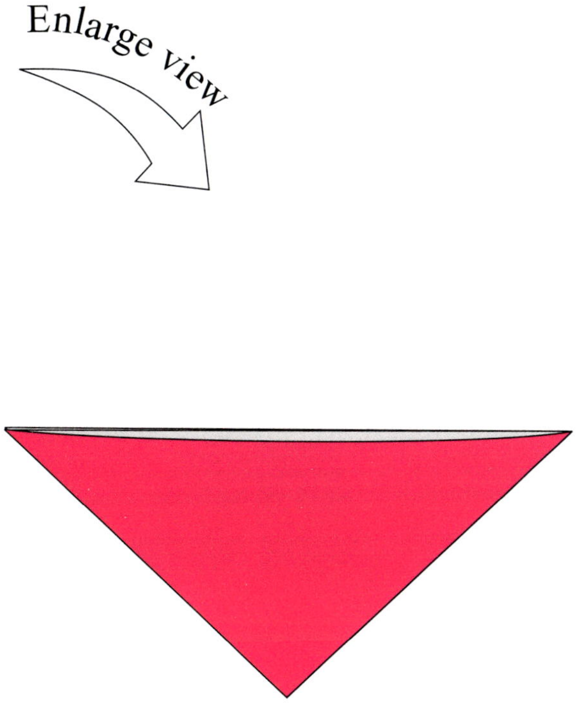

5 .... like this.

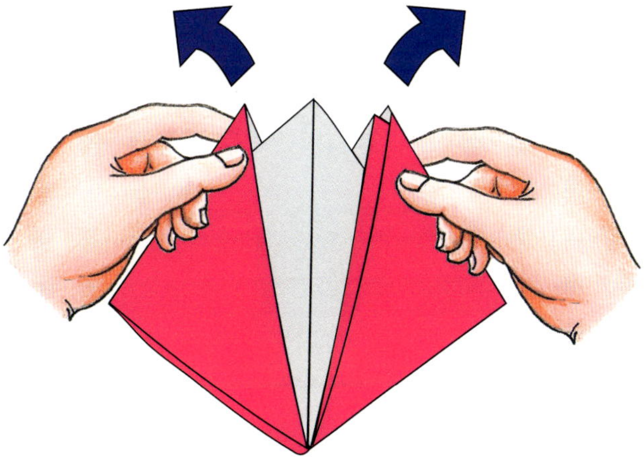

7 Pull out the flaps gently from both the sides and flatten to form the boat.

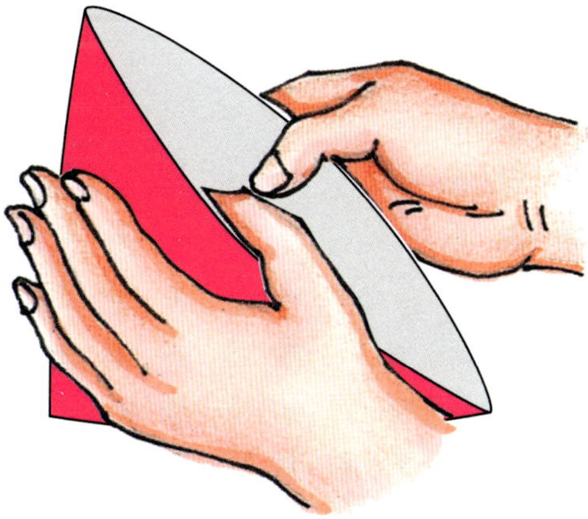

6 Insert your thumbs in, and open out the model. Flatten it to form a square.

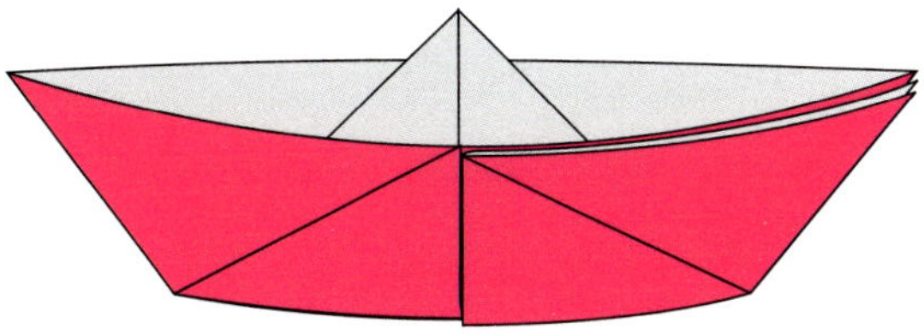

8 Your boat is ready.

Necktie

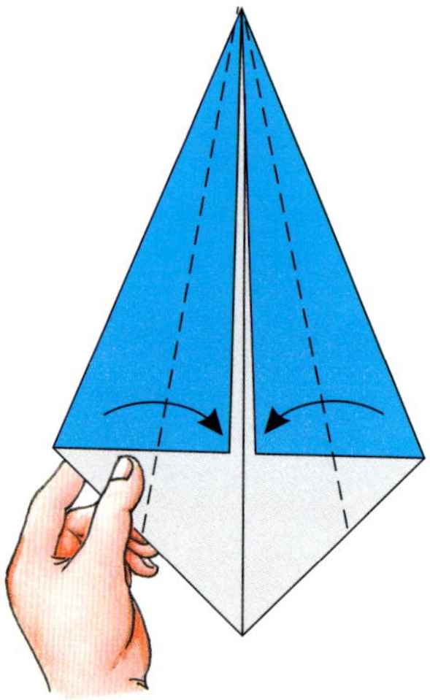

2 Again fold both the sides inside along the dotted lines.

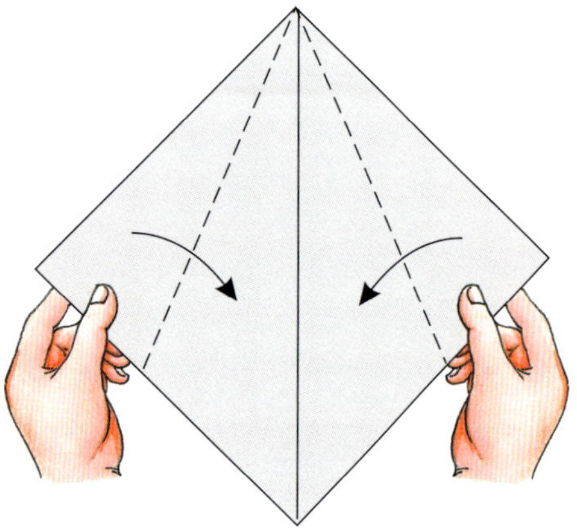

1 Make the centre crease and fold along the dotted lines.

3 Again fold along the dotted lines.

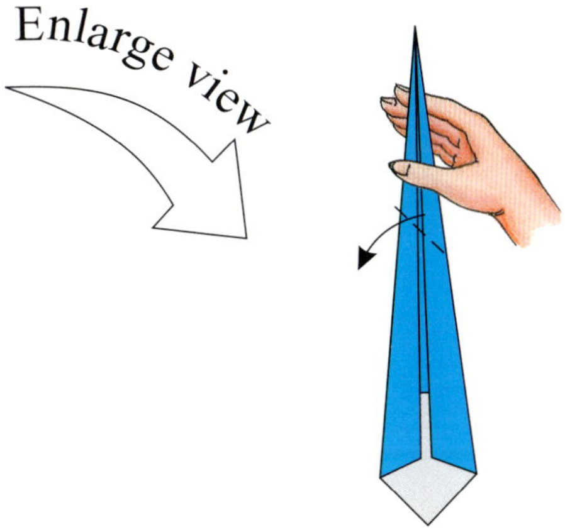

4 Fold the top corner downwards along the dotted line.

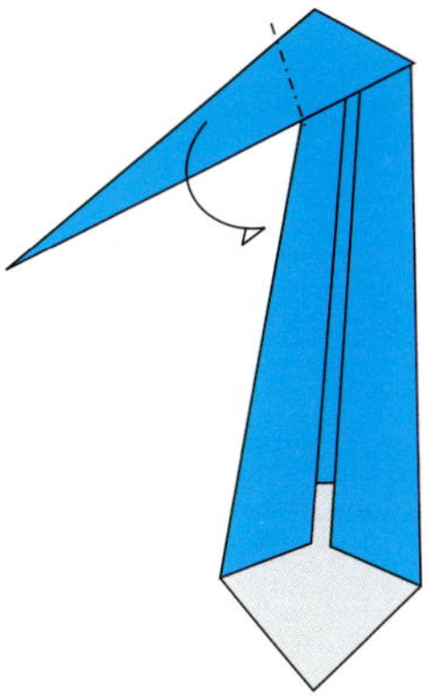

5 Again fold it backward in the direction of arrow.

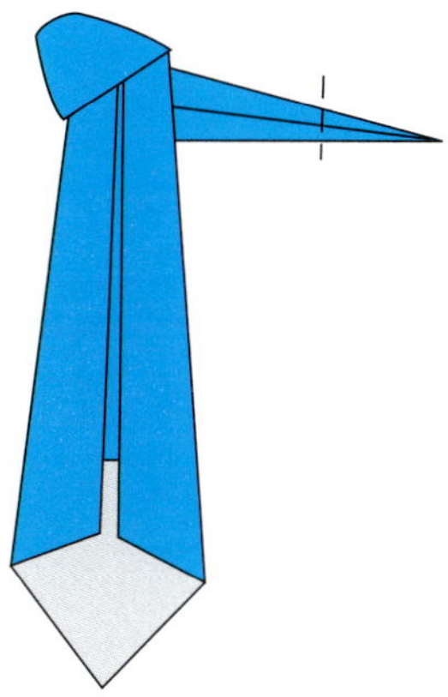

6 Make a fold on the dotted line.

7 Fold it inside in the direction of arrow....

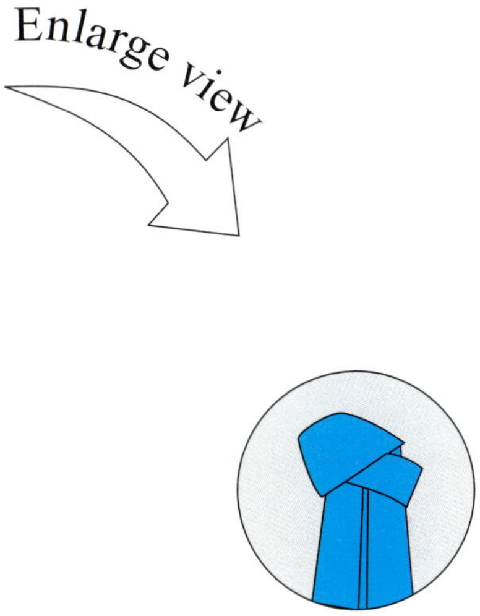

8 ....like this.

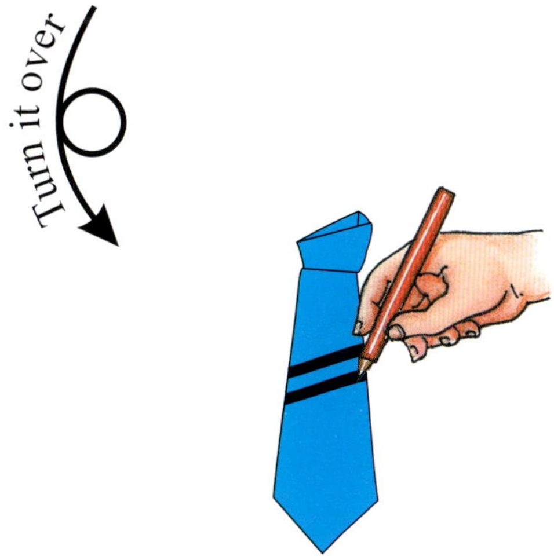

9 Decorate your necktie with the colourful stripes.

Fish

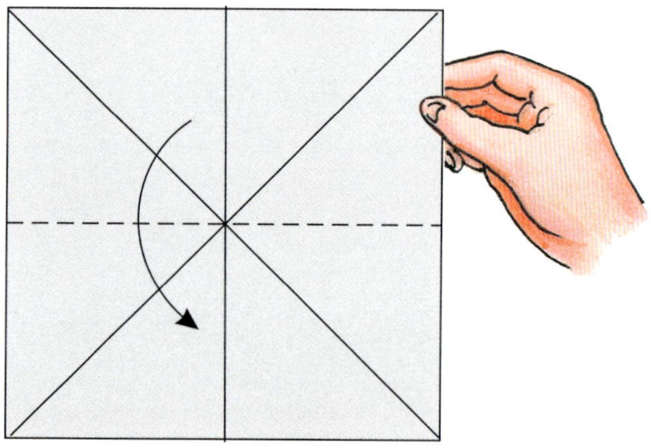

2 Fold along the dotted line.

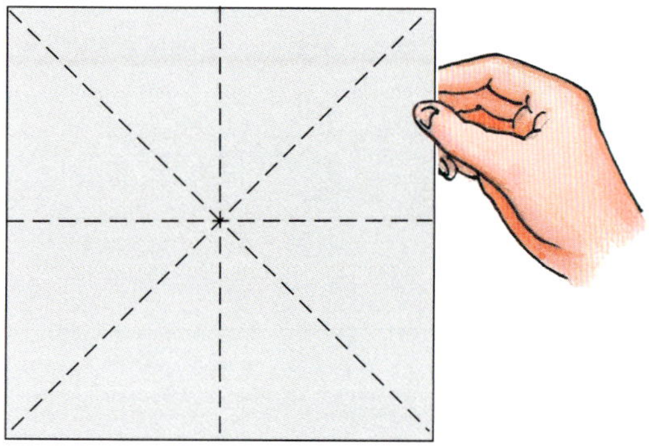

1 Fold the paper along the dotted lines and unfold it.

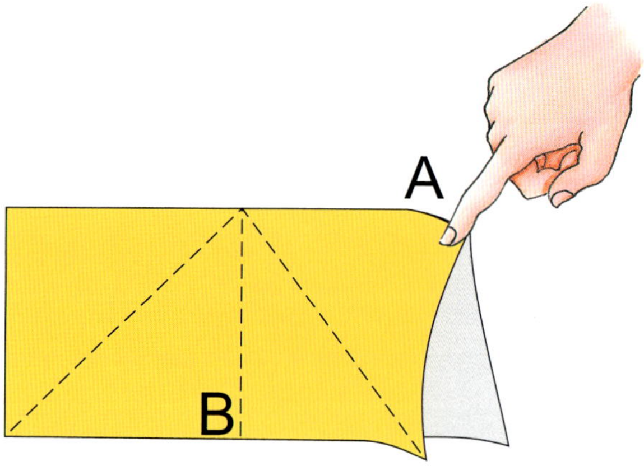

3 Push right side at the point 'A' down inside of the form to meet point 'B'.

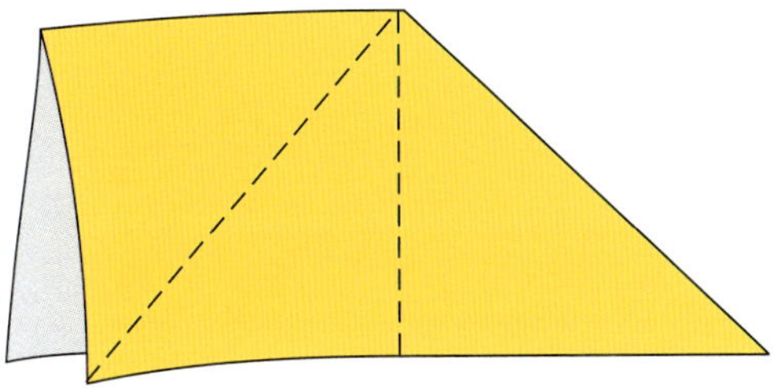

4 Repeat the previous step with the left side also.

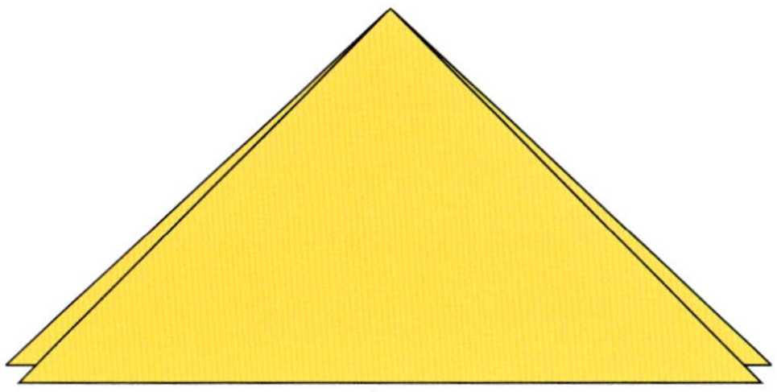

5 Your form will now look like this.

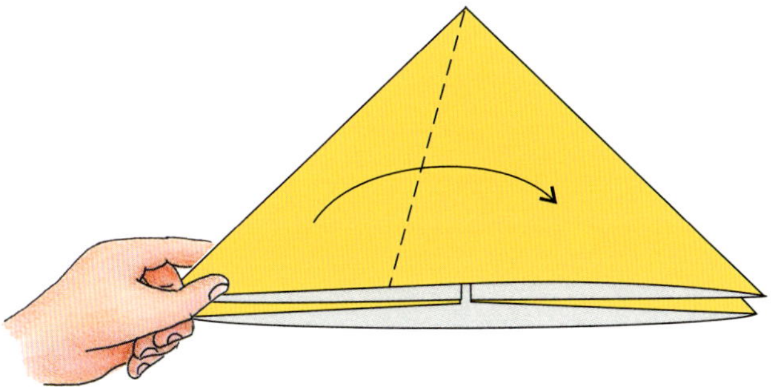

6 Fold the left corner of the upper layer to the right side along the dotted line.

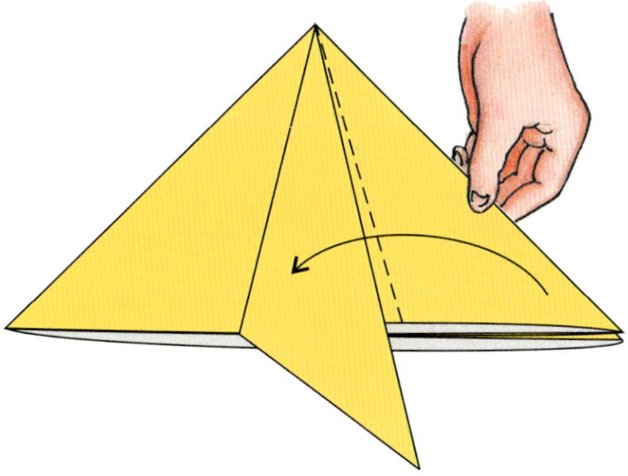

7 Fold the right corner of the upper layer to overlap the left flap....

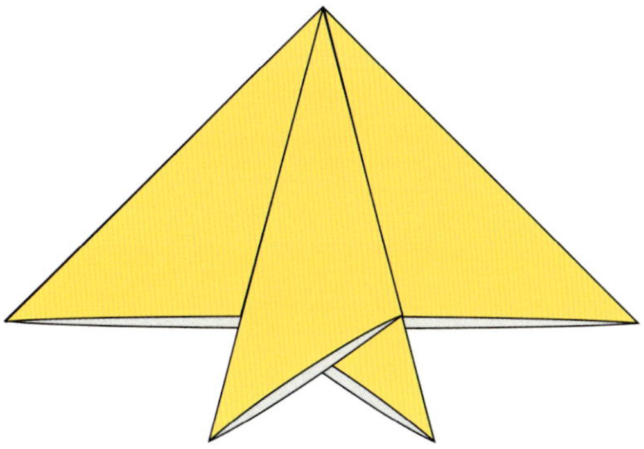

8 ...like this.

9 Draw an eye and make your fish smiling.

Multi Purpose Basket

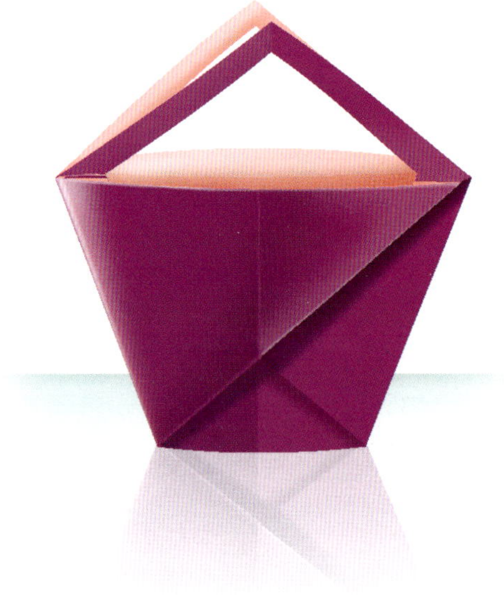

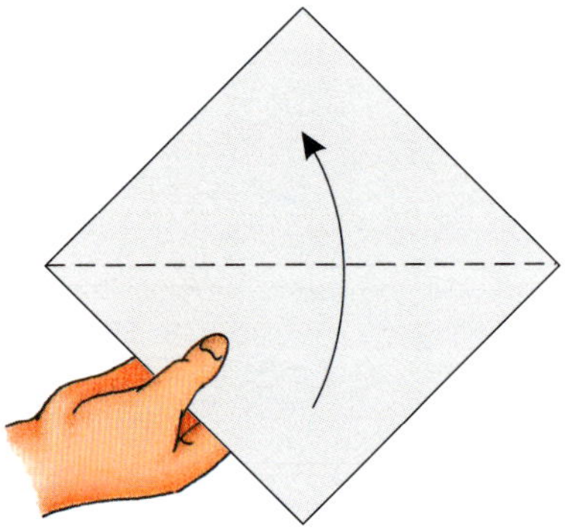

1 Fold in half along the dotted line.

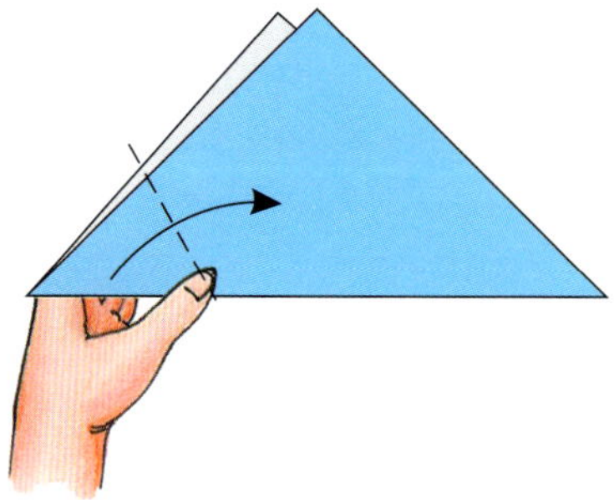

2 Fold the left corner along the dotted line.

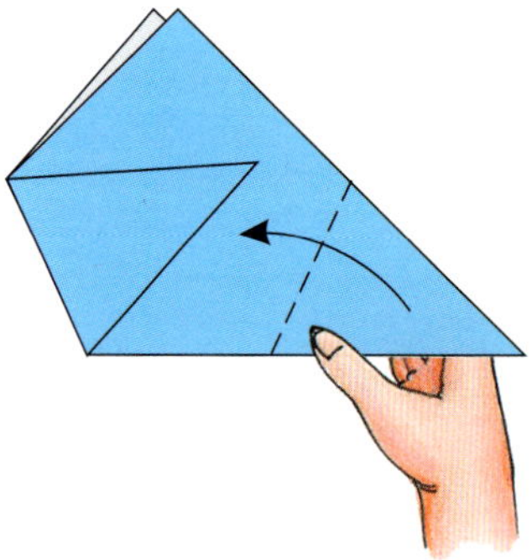

3 Fold the right corner along the dotted line.

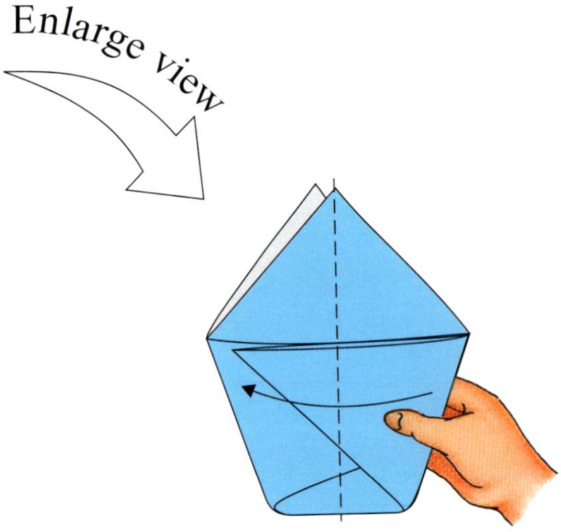

4 Fold the form in half in the direction of arrow.

5 Make a cut as shown and open the middle fold.

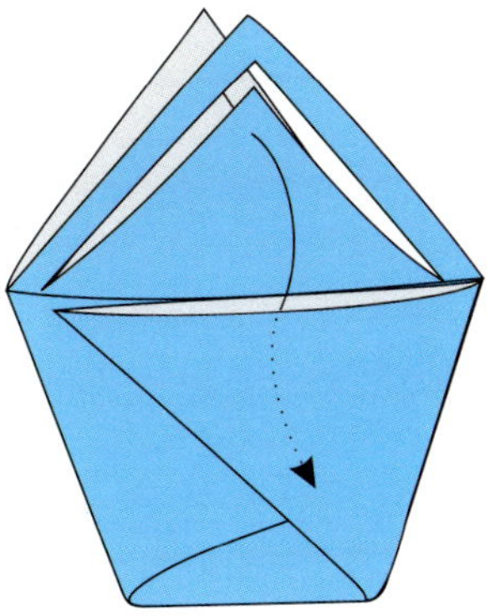

6 Fold the upper flap forward and slide it inside the pocket....

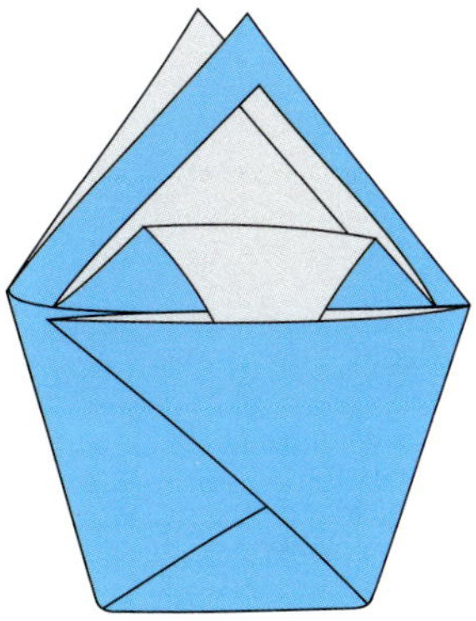

7 ..... like this.

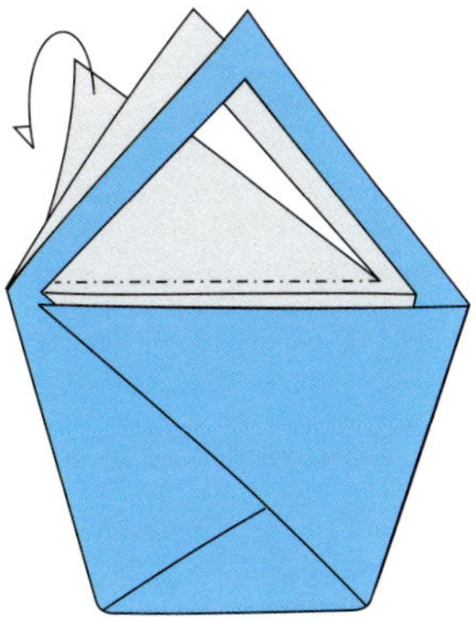

8 Fold the second flap backwards as shown.

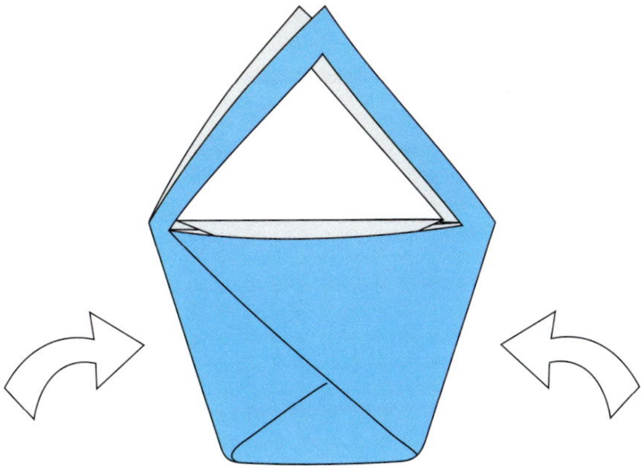

9 Press gently from both the sides to give a proper shape to the basket.

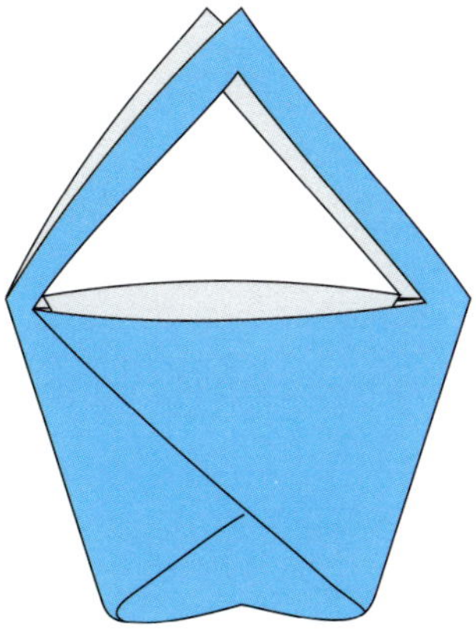

10 Now, your basket is ready to hold your sweets, flowers, etc.

Pigeon

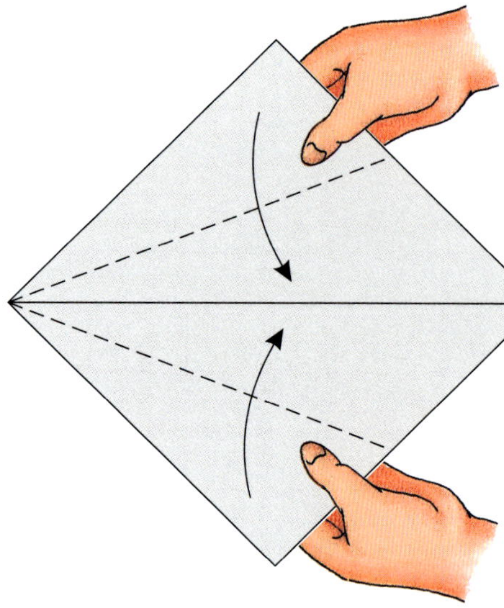

2 Fold the top and the bottom corners along the dotted lines.

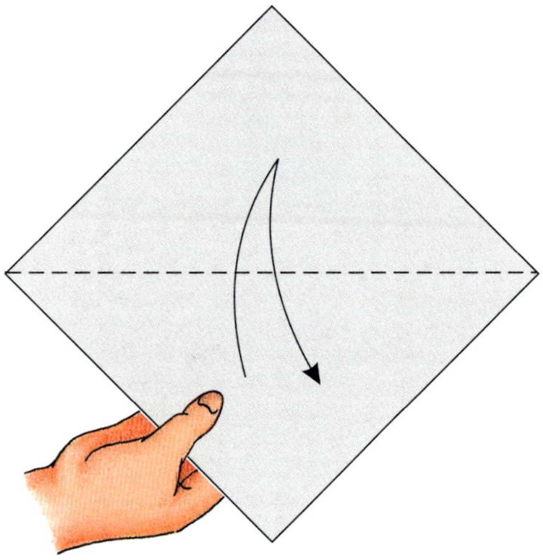

1 Fold the paper in half and unfold it.

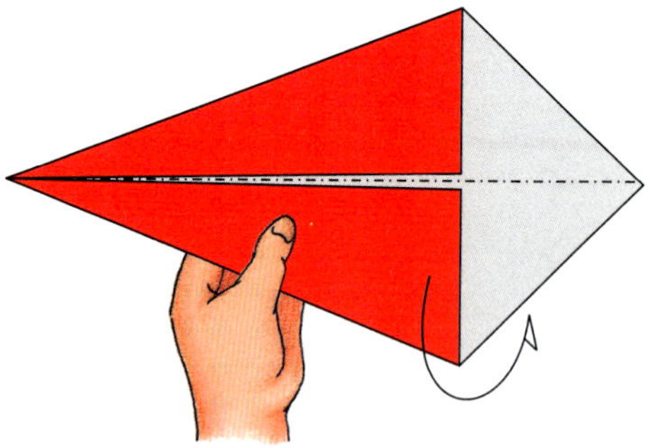

3 Fold backwards in half along the dotted line.

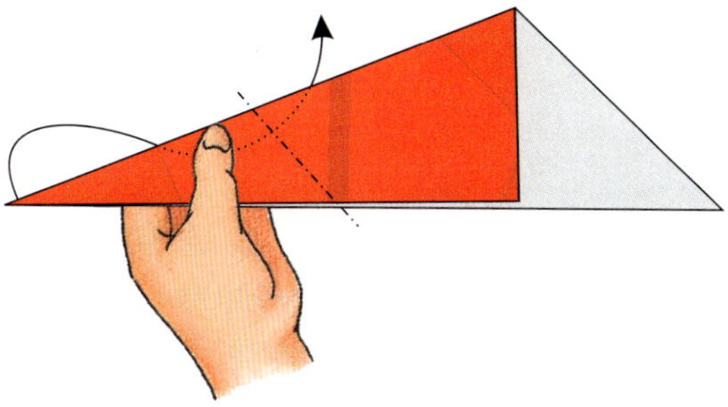

4 Make a pocket fold to form the bird's neck.

Again make a pocket fold towards the left side for the head.

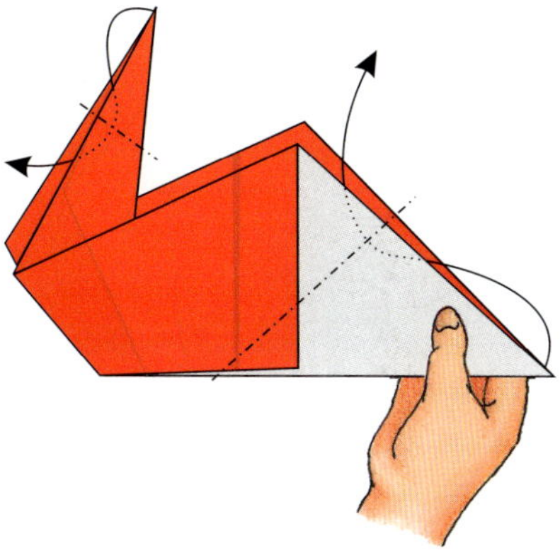

5 Make another pocket fold at the right side for the tail.

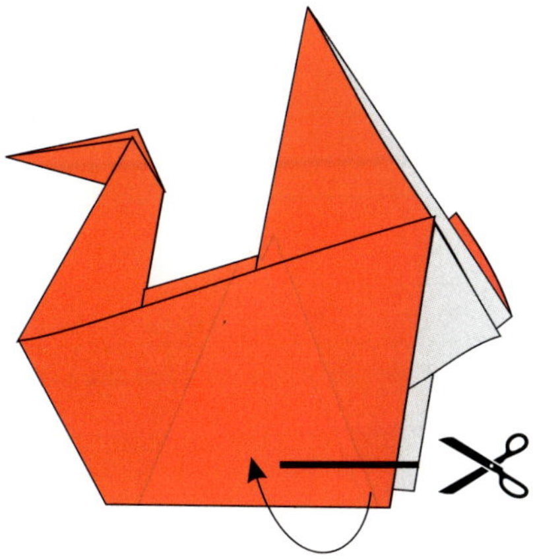

6 Make a cut and fold the flaps to form the legs.

7 The pigeon is ready.

Butterfly

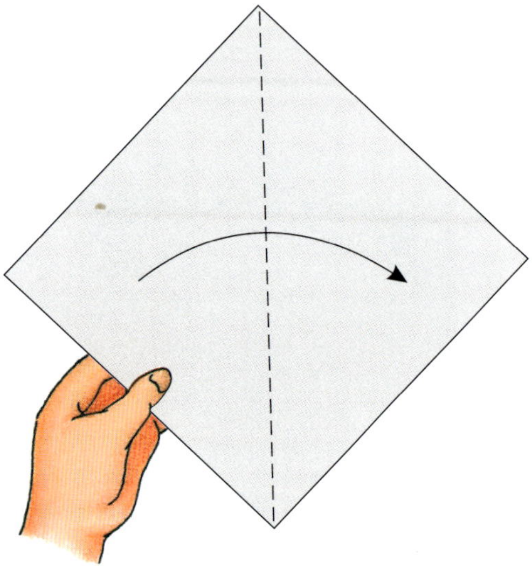

1 Make a centre crease and fold it.

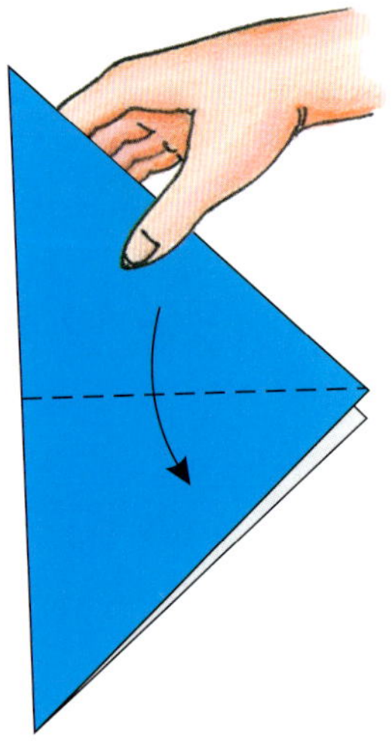

2 Fold along the dotted line in the direction of arrow.

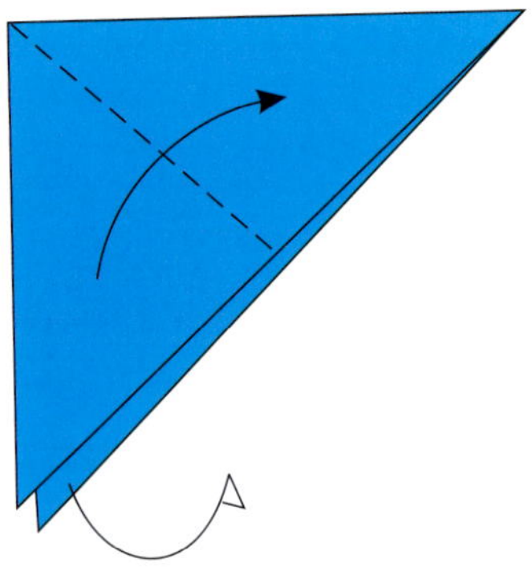

3 Fold both the lower flaps upwards in the direction of arrows.

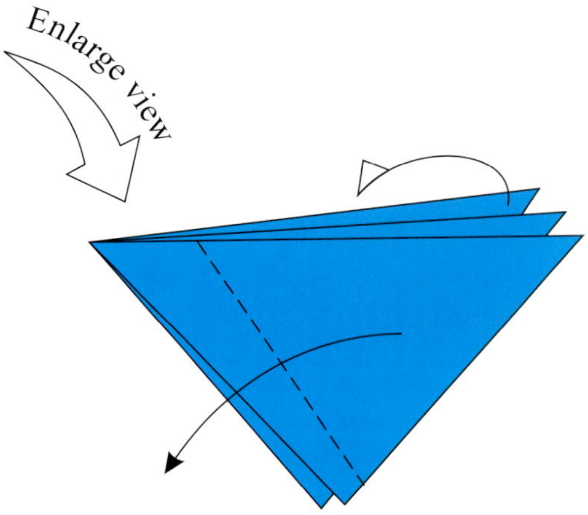

4 Now fold the front and the back flap downward along the dotted line.

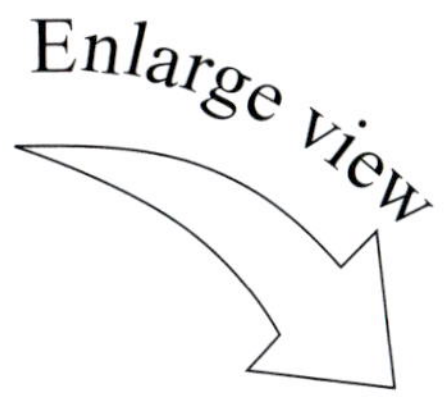

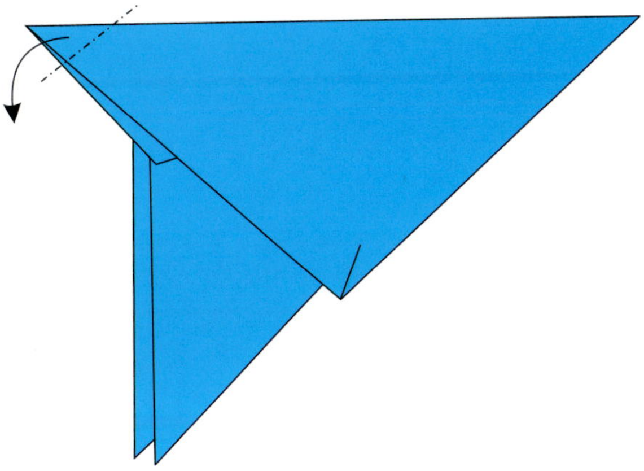

5 Make the pocket fold along the dotted line.

7 Fold both the sides upward along the dotted line.

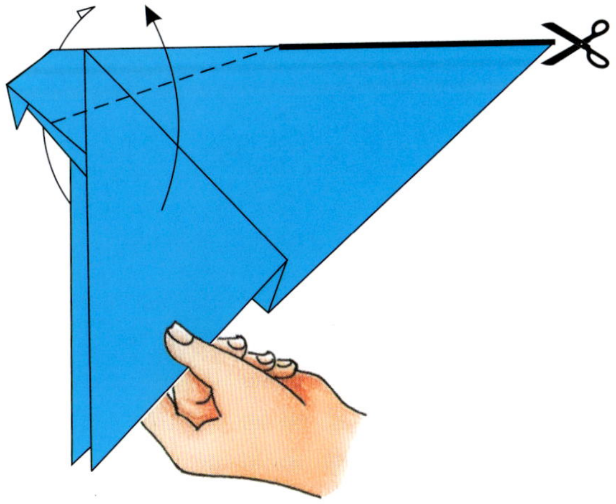

6 Cut the marked portion and fold upward along the dotted line from both the sides.

8 Open the wings and decorate them. Your butterfly is ready.

Elephant

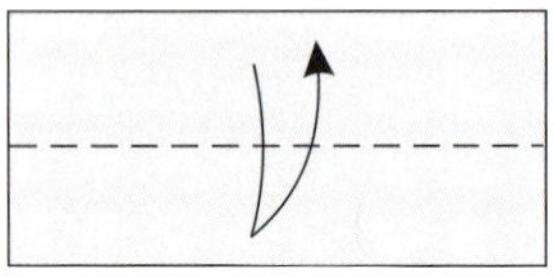

1 Use rectangular sheet. Fold and then unfold along the dotted line.

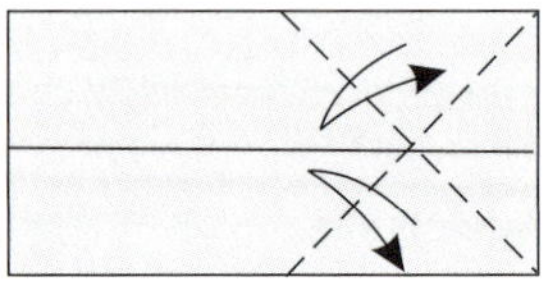

2 Fold and unfold along both the dotted lines alternately.

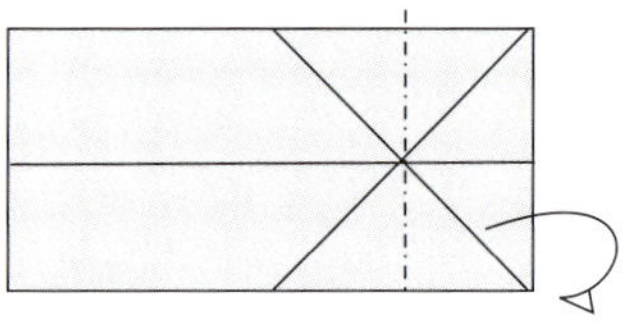

3 Fold backwards, make a crease and unfold.

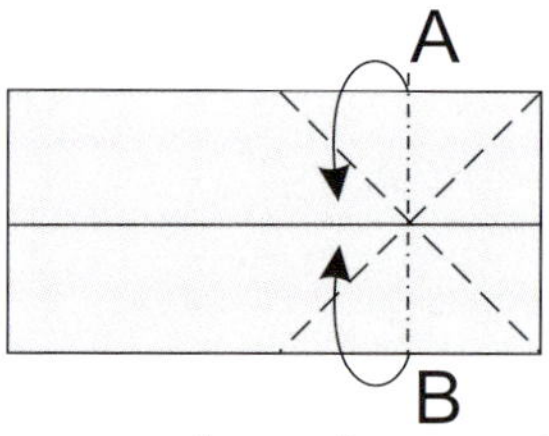

4 Fold outer edges in, so that the points 'A' and 'B' will meet each other at the centre line.

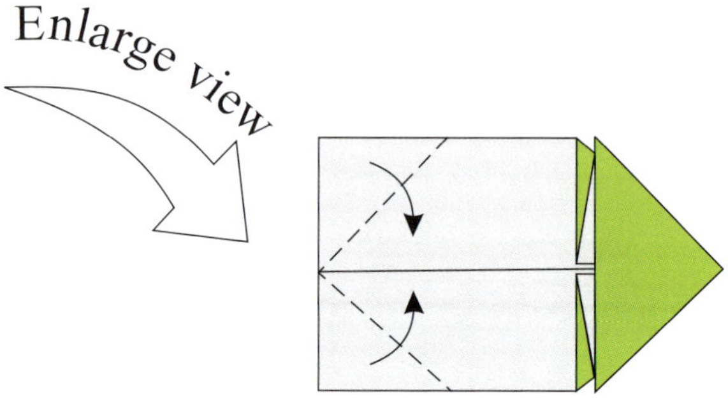

5 Make folds inside along the dotted lines.

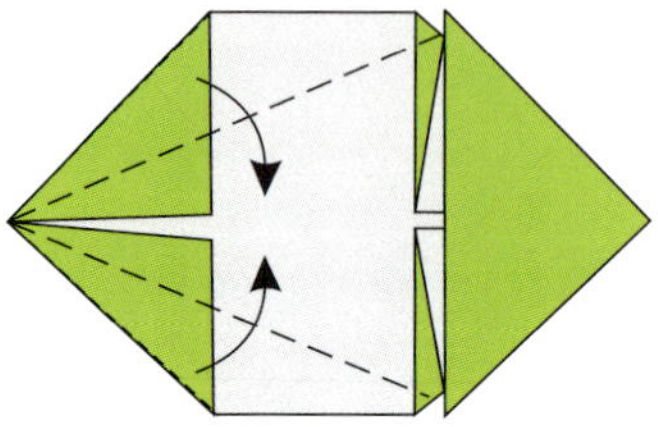

6 Again fold both the flaps inside in the direction of arrows.

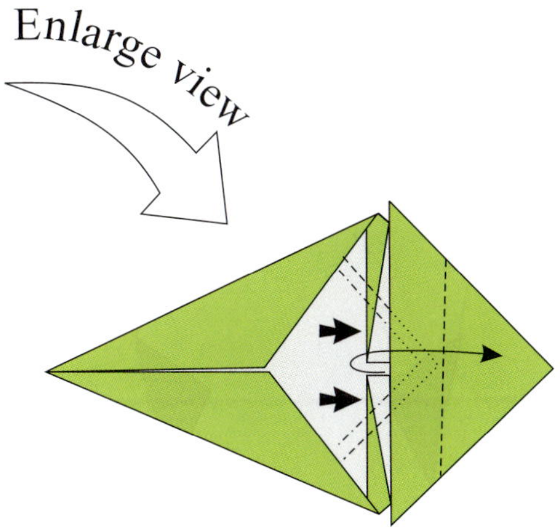

7 Open the upper right flap along the dotted line while creasing centre corners.

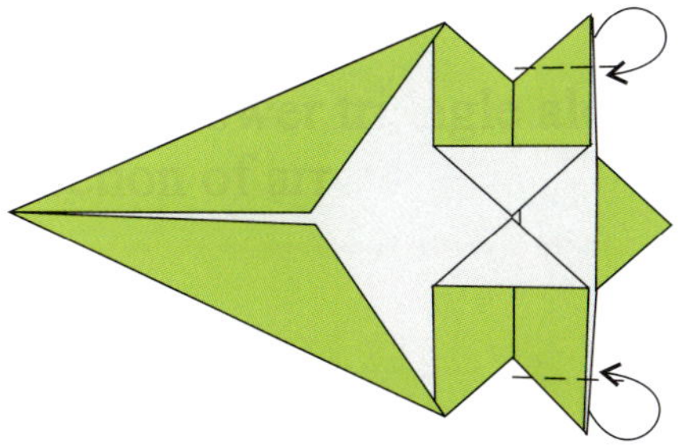

8 Fold both the corners inside as shown.

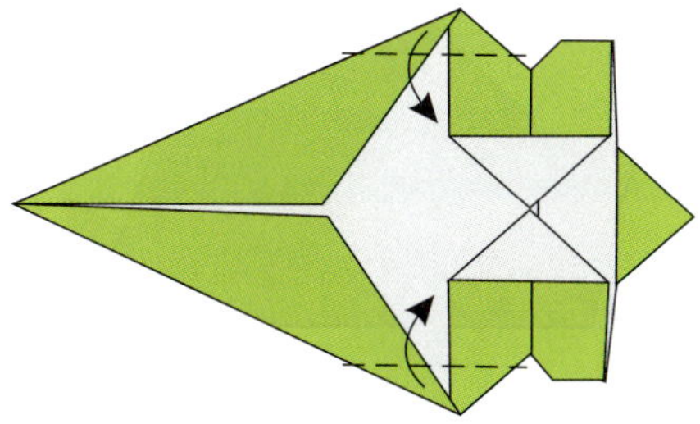

9 Fold the top and bottom corners inside in the direction of arrows.

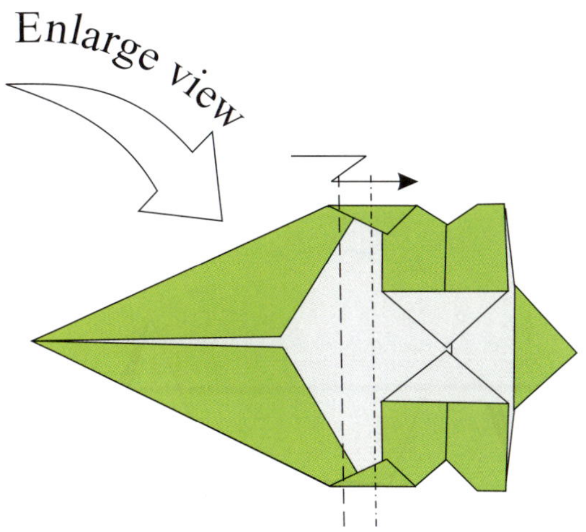

10 Make stair-step fold in the direction of arrow.

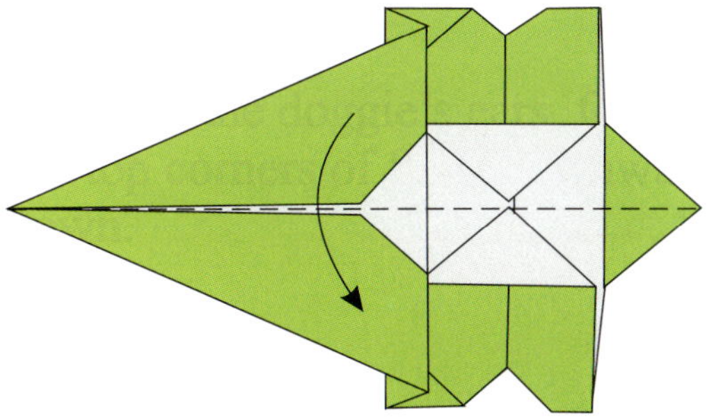

11 Fold the form in half.

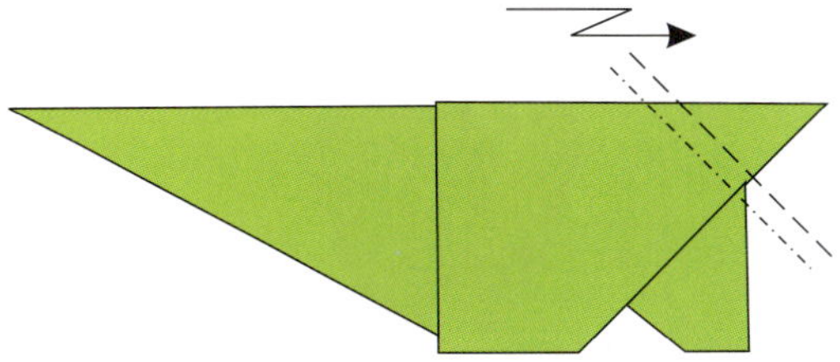

12 Fold forward and backward along the dotted lines and make a stair-step fold at the right-corner.

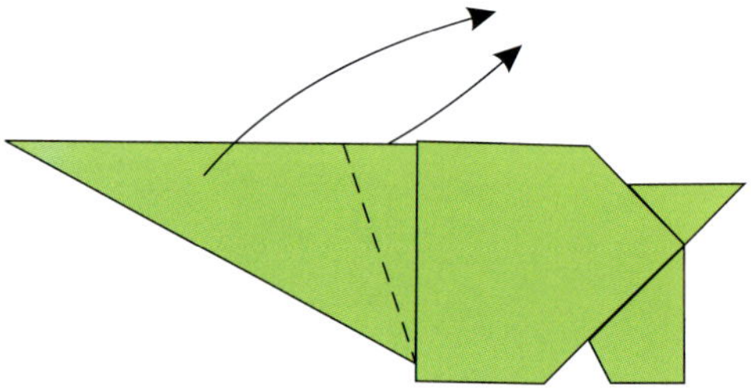

13 Make a hood fold along the dotted line in the direction of arrows.

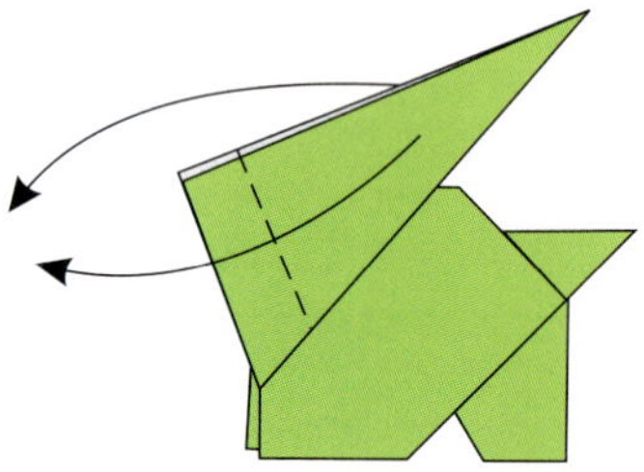

14 Again fold the top flap downwards along the dotted line.

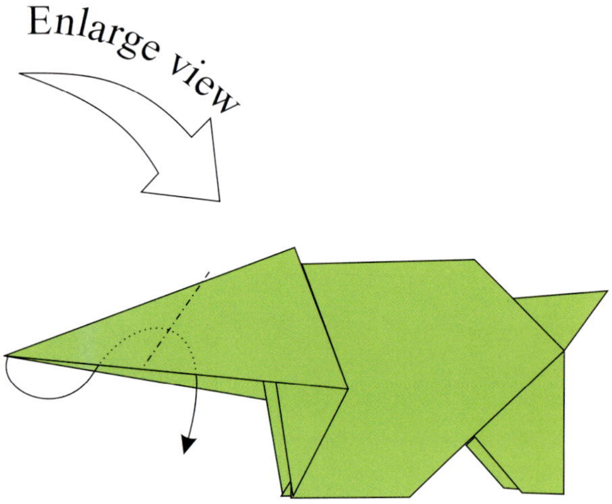

15 So your form will look like this. Now make a pocket fold along the dotted line in the downward direction.

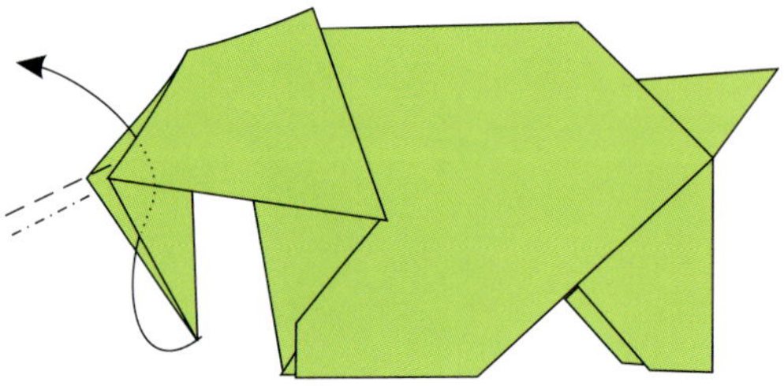

16 Make a pocket fold along the dotted line.

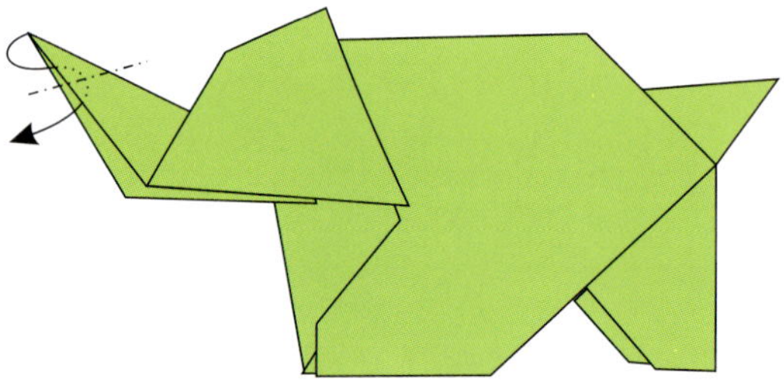

17 Again make a pocket fold along the dotted line.

18 Draw eyes and your elephant is ready.

Collage Work

Multi Purpose Basket

TIPS AND TRICKS

Step-1 Collect paper sheets of various colours of your own choice. Tear them in small pieces of different shapes.

Step-2 Set them within the outline and paste in the given shape.

Cut and Paste

Necktie

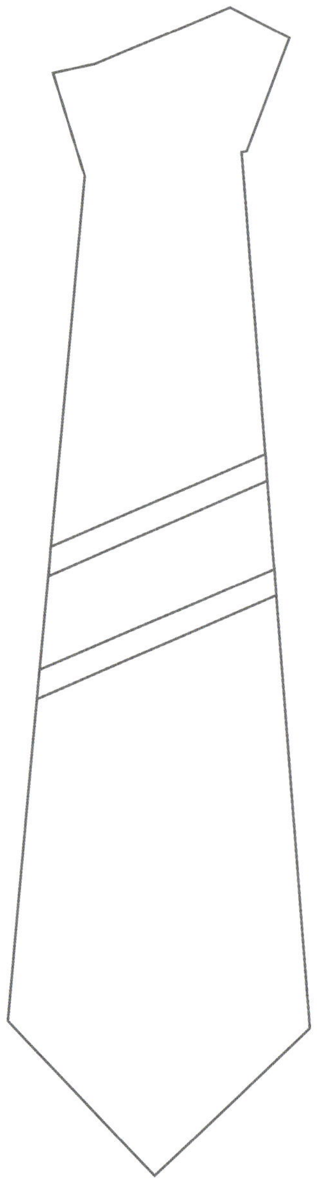

TIPS AND TRICKS

Step-1 Take craft paper sheets of various colours. Trace different parts on the shape of different colours.

Step-2 Now paste these pieces at the appropriate places.

Crushed Paper Art

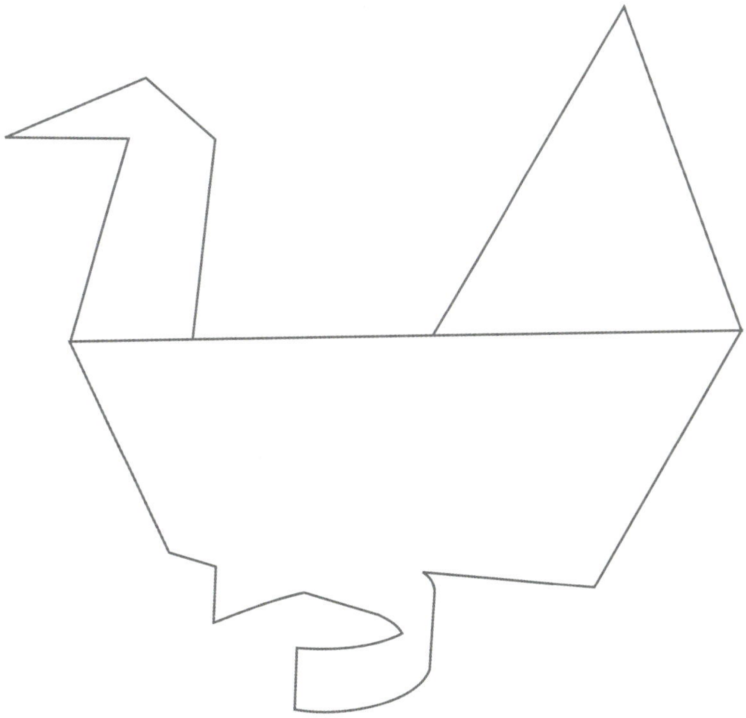

Pigeon

TIPS AND TRICKS

Step-1 Take a plain paper and squeeze it in your hand. Open it gently and apply the poster colour with a flat brush.

Step-2 Now cut the paper according to the shape and paste it within the outline.

Spray Paint

Butterfly

TIPS AND TRICKS

Step-1 Take a white paper. Spray different colours of your own choice with a tooth brush on the white paper.

Step-2 Cut the parts of the shape as per your liking and paste them on the figure.

Yacht

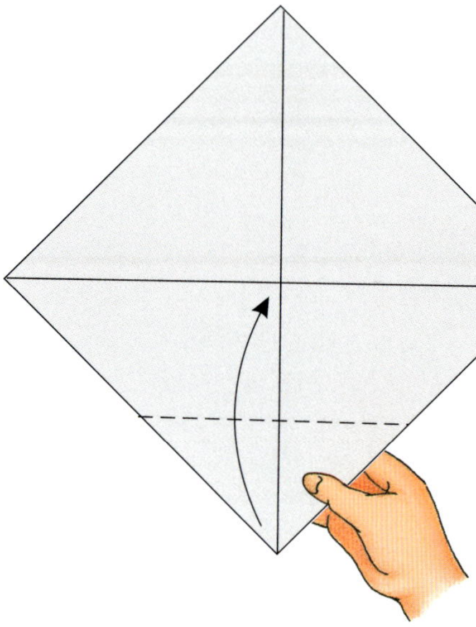

1 Find the centre of the paper. Fold the lower tip along the dotted line to the centre.

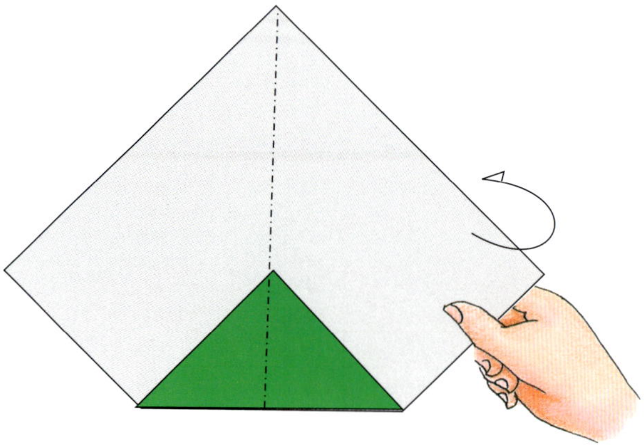

2 Fold in half backwards along the dotted line.

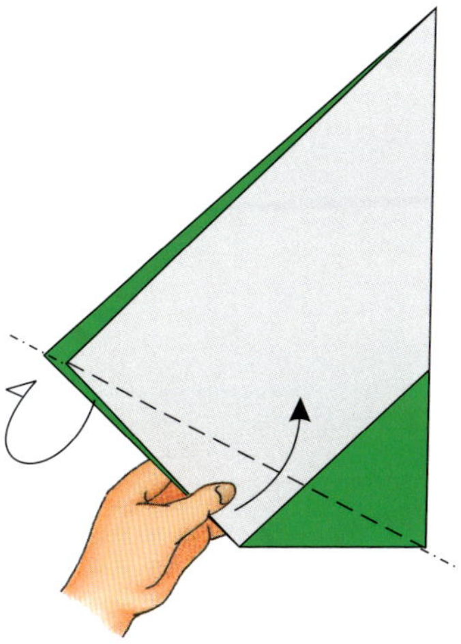

3 Fold the upper layer upward and the lower layer backward as shown.

4 Pull out the triangular flap, as shown to form the body of the yacht.

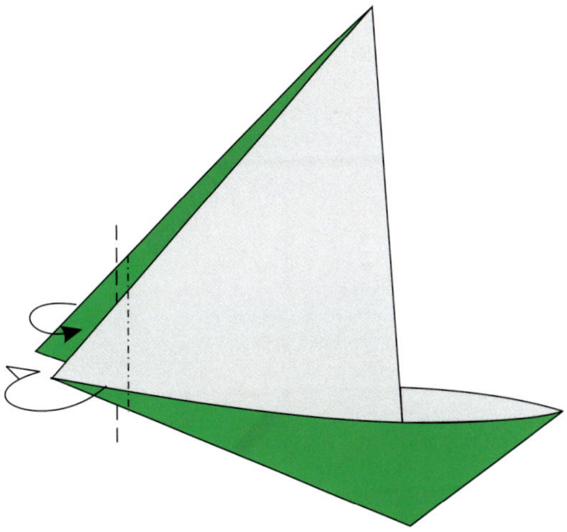

5 Fold both the left corners inside along the dotted line to give proper shape to the sail.

6 Paint bright stripes on both the sides of the sail. Now see, how lovely the yacht looks.

Rooster

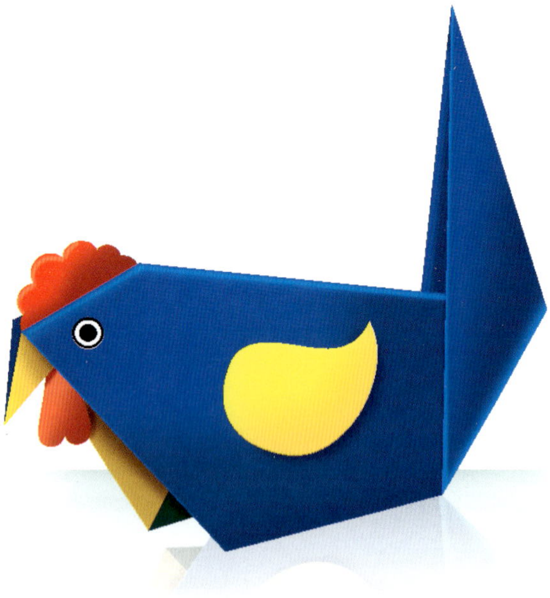

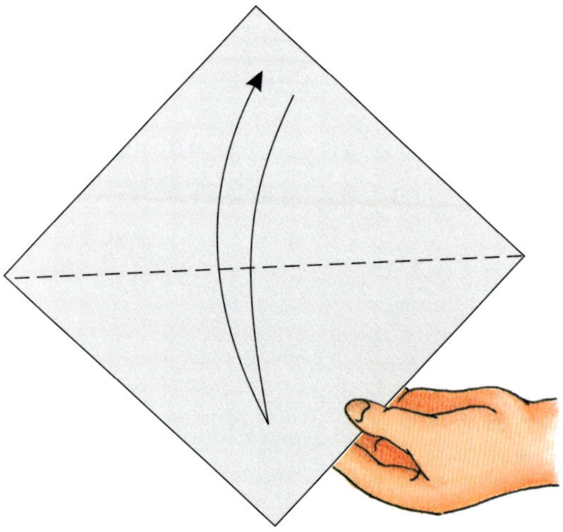

1 Make a centre crease and unfold it.

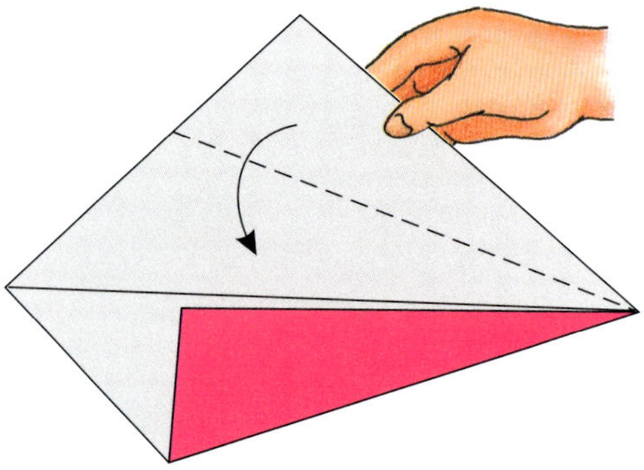

2 Fold the top and the bottom corners to the centre crease.

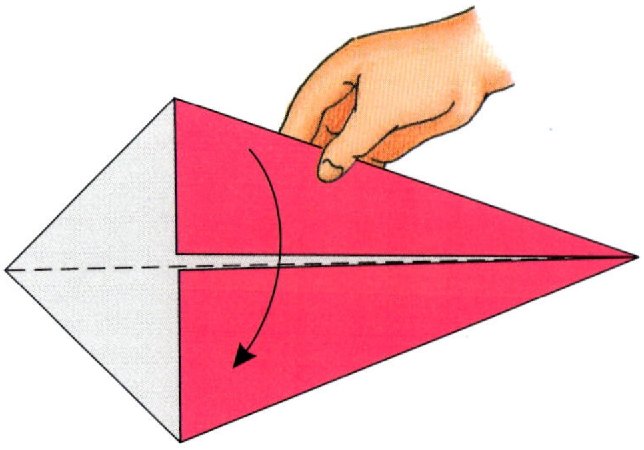

3 Again fold in half along the dotted line.

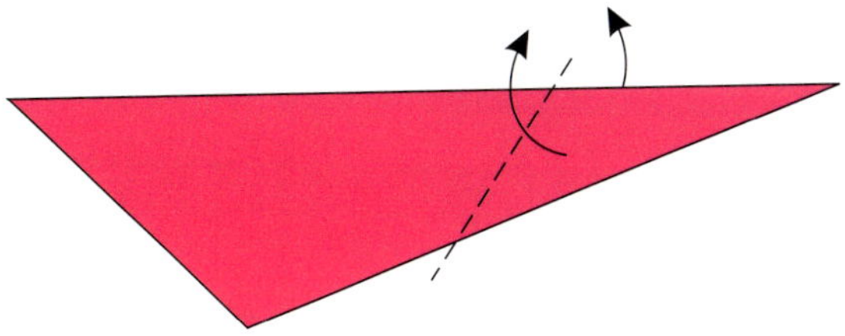

4 Make a hood fold along the dotted line in the direction of arrows.

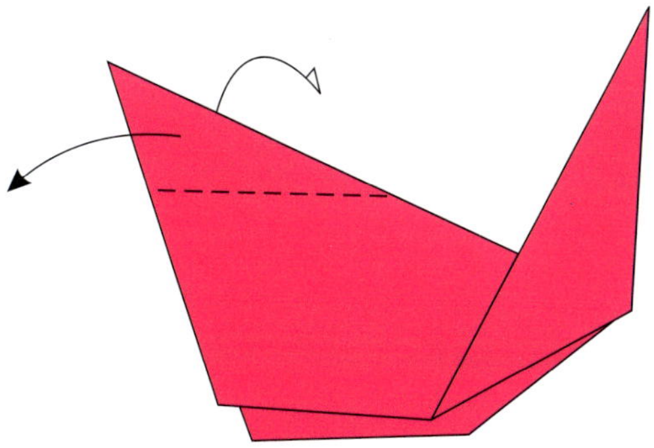

5 Make a pocket fold along the dotted line (fold forward and backward and unfold it....

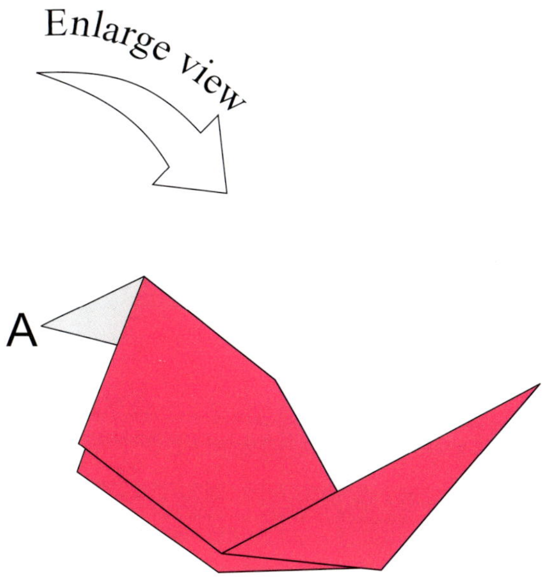

6 ....open the form slightly and thrust the point "A" inside) to form the beak of the rooster.

7 Draw eyes and wings, and paste a paper crown on it's head.

King Cobra

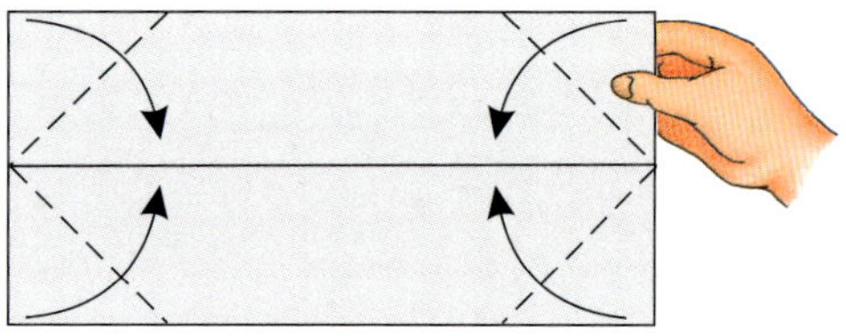

1 Use one half of the paper and fold all the four corners to the centre line along the dotted lines.

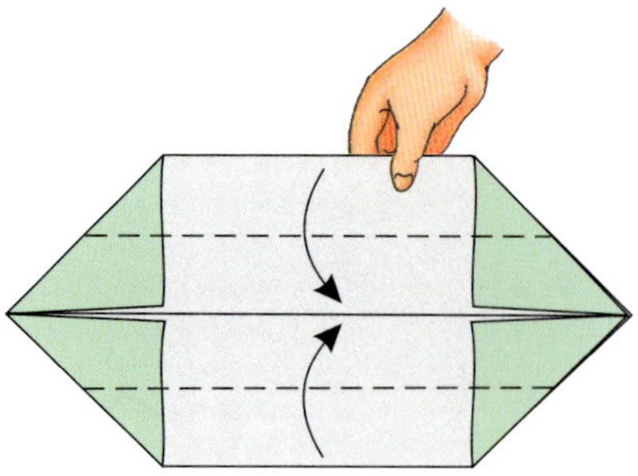

2 Fold the top and the bottom sides to the centre line.

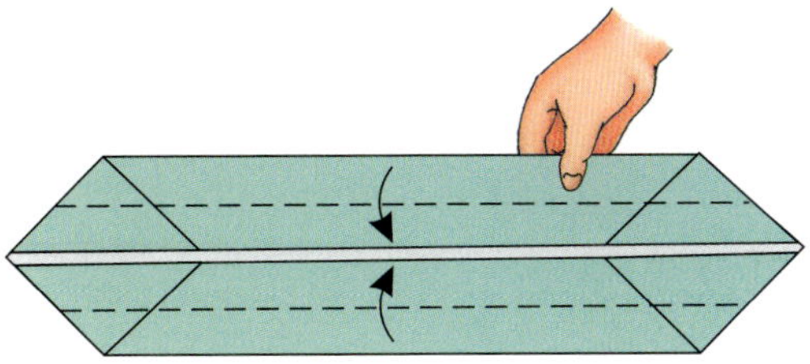

3 Once again fold the top and the bottom sides to the centre line.

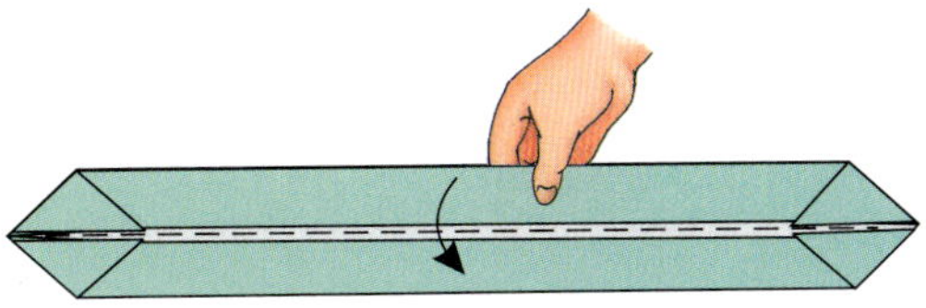

4 Fold the form in half along the dotted line.

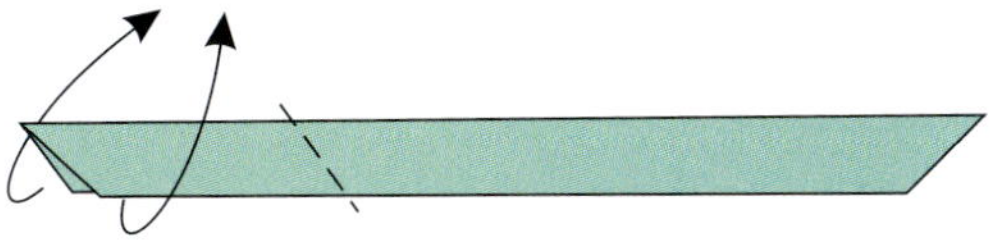

5 Make a hood fold backwards along the dotted line.

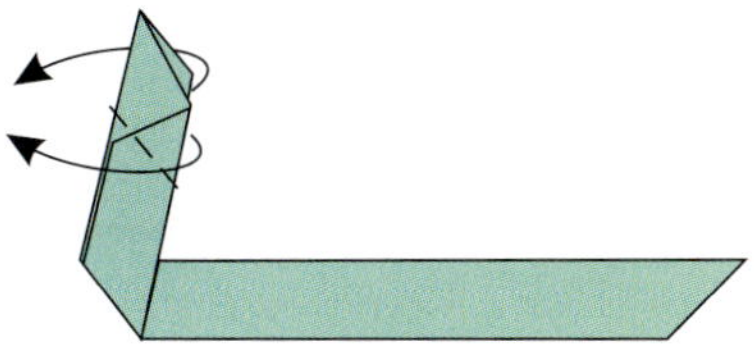

6 Make a hood fold forward once again for the snake's hood.

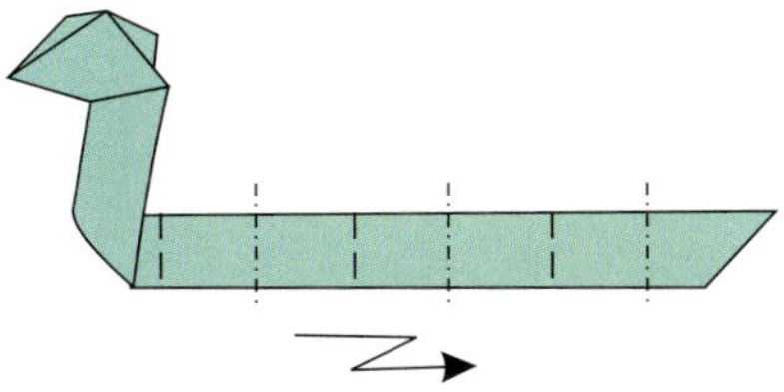

7 Make a stair-step fold by folding forward and backwards alternately for the snake's body.

8 Draw eyes and dots on the body and the cobra is ready.

Bat Mask

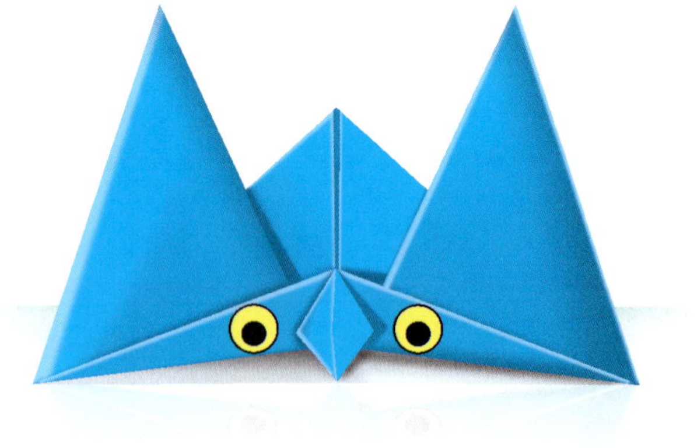

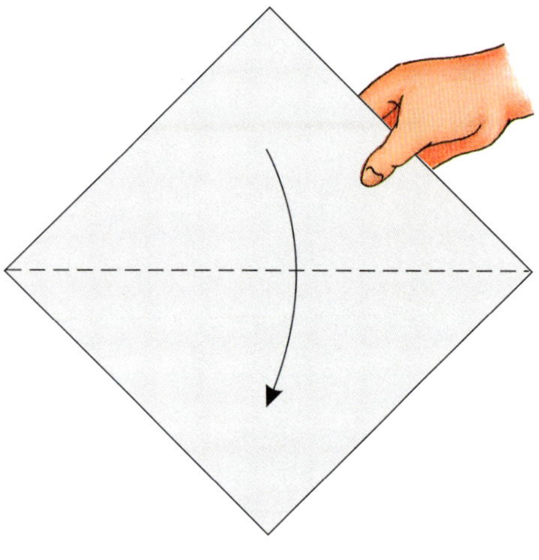

1 Fold in half in the direction of arrow.

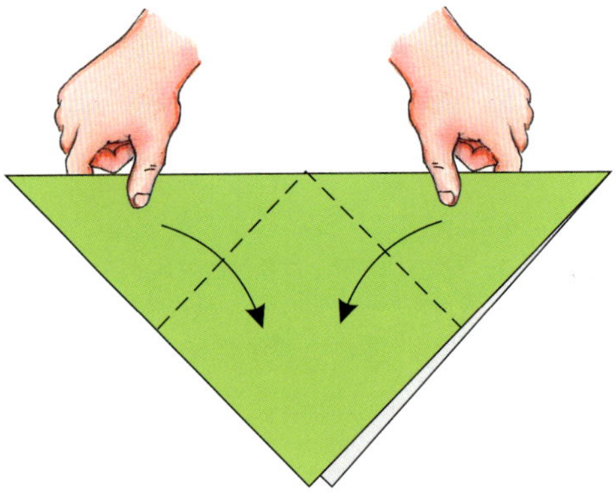

2 Fold inside along the dotted lines.

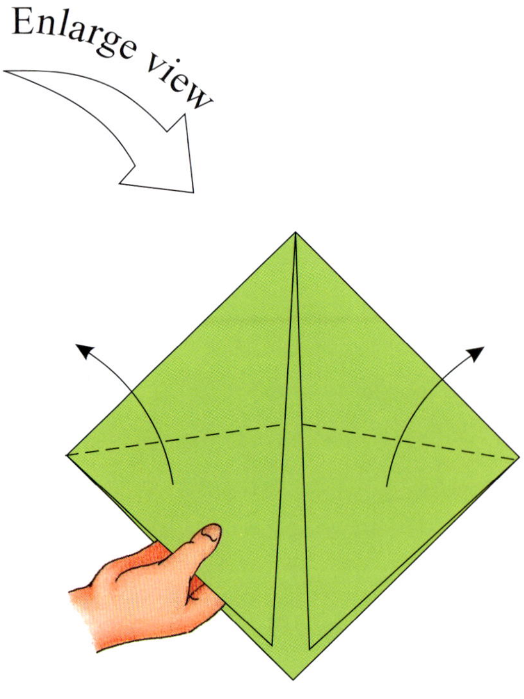

3 Fold both the flaps upwards.

4 Make a valley fold for front layer and mountain fold for back layer.

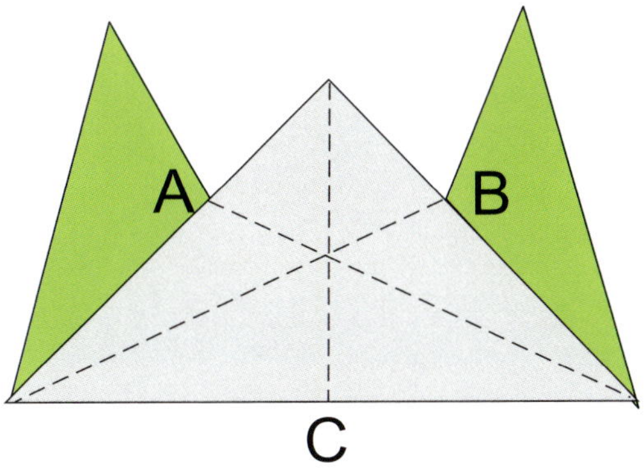

5 Fold then unfold the front flap along the dotted lines and bring down 'A' and 'B' together to meet at 'C'. Nose will appear at once.

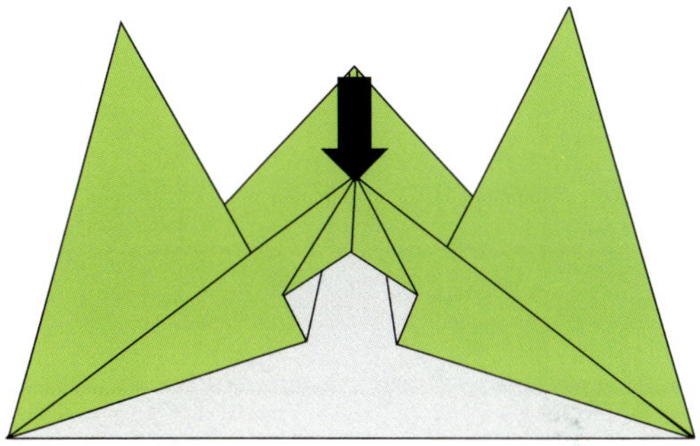

6 Press the nose with your thumb.

7 Draw eyes.

Joker

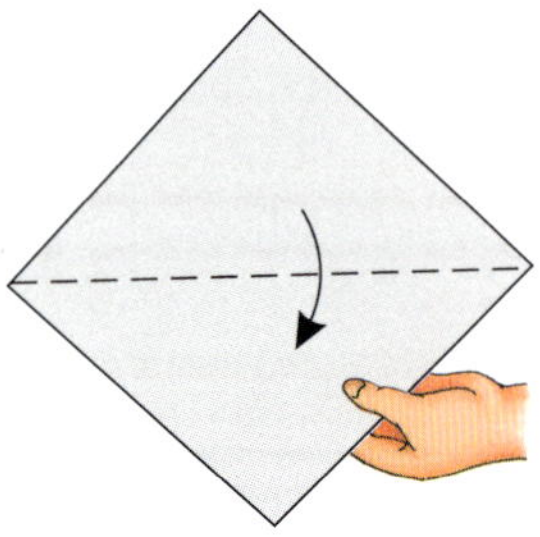

1 Fold in half.

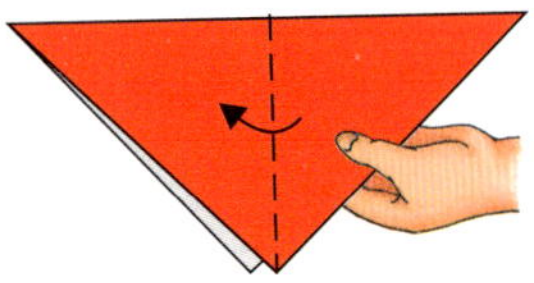

2 Again fold in the direction of arrow.

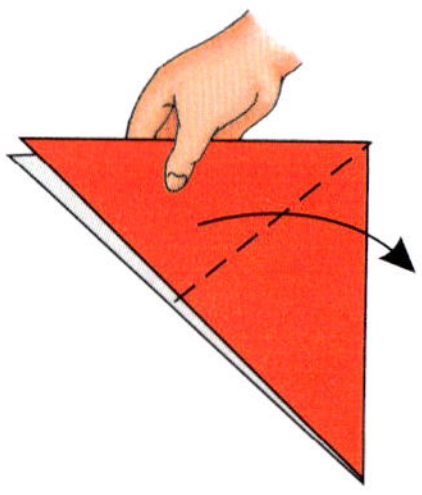

3 Fold the upper flap downwards along the dotted line.

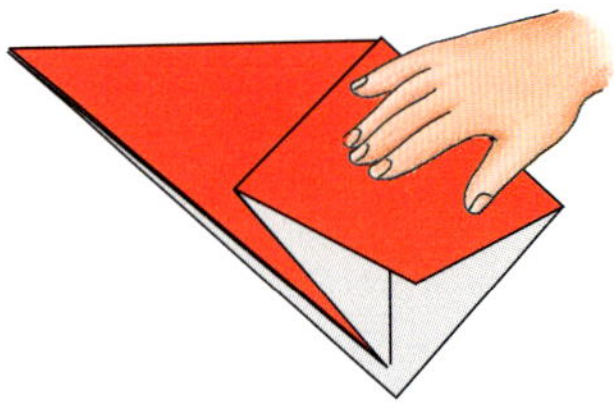

4 Now open the flap and press it to flatten it. Fold the back side in the same way.

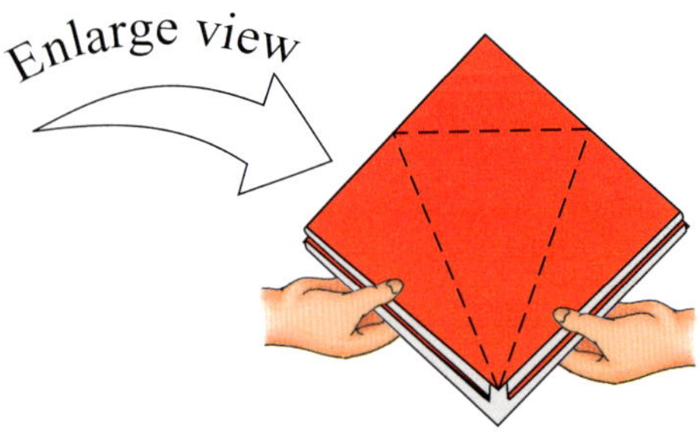

5 Your form will look like this. Make all the creases along the dotted lines and then unfold them.

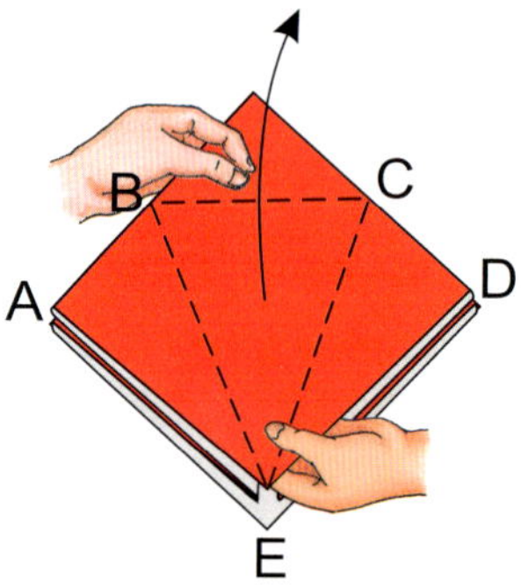

6 Press the upper portion of the form and pull the top flap upward along the dotted line B--------C.

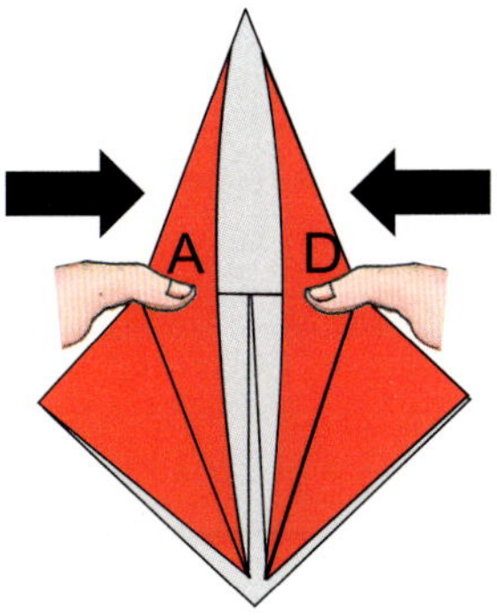

7 While pulling upward the top flap, press both thumbs at points ‘A’ and ‘D’ so that they meet at the centre of the form.

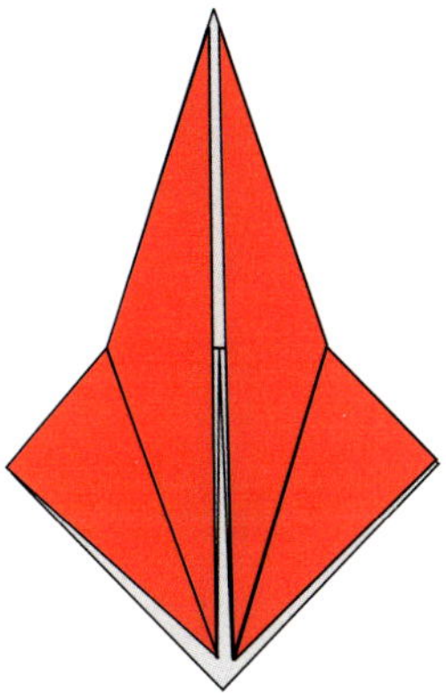

8 Your form will look like this. Now fold the back side in the same way.

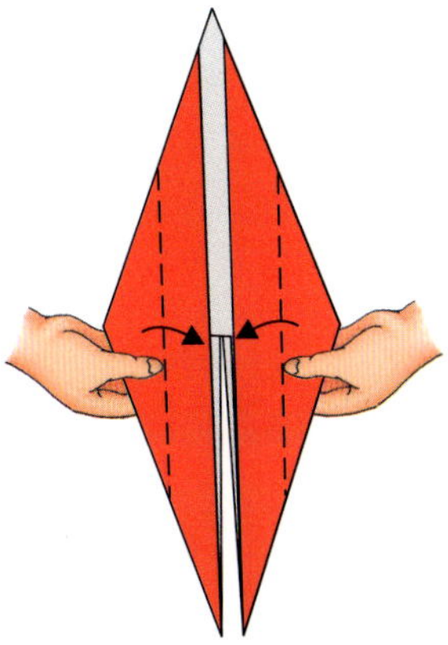

9 Fold the right and left corners to the centre along the dotted lines. Fold the back side in the same way.

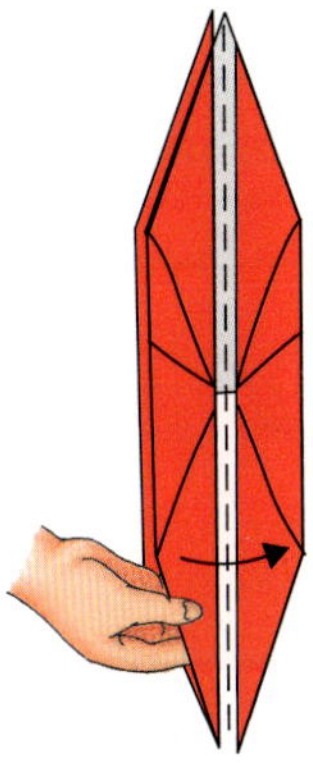

10 Fold the left half over the right half along the dotted line. Make the same fold at the backside also. Turn upside down.

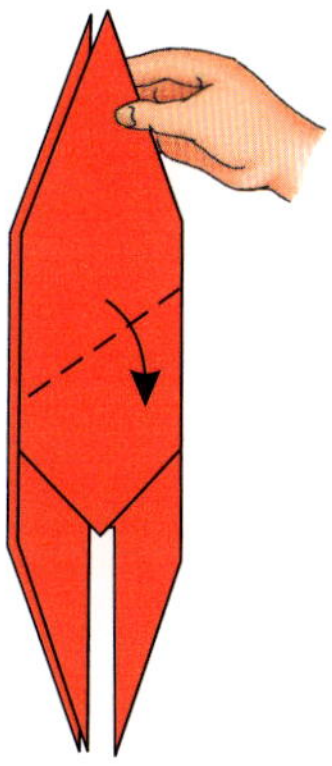

11 Fold the front flap along the dotted line.

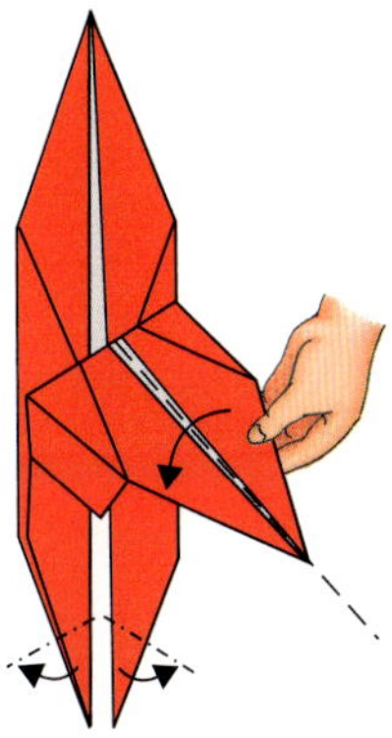

12 Fold the same flap over its half portion along the dotted line and make pocket folds at both the bottom ends.

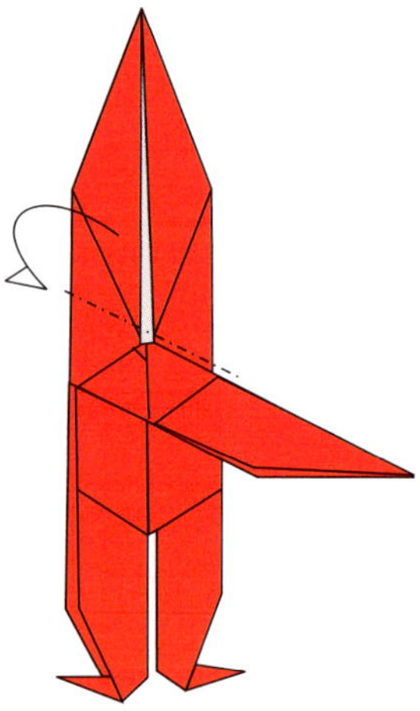

13 Now fold the back flap backwards along the dotted line.

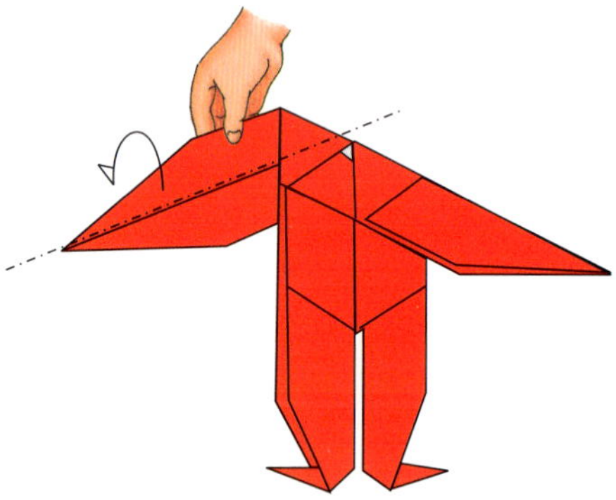

14 Now fold the back flap along the dotted line downwardly.

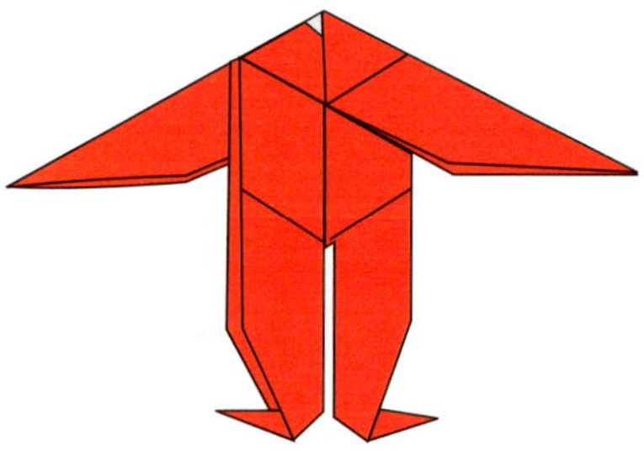

15 Your final form of the body will look like this.

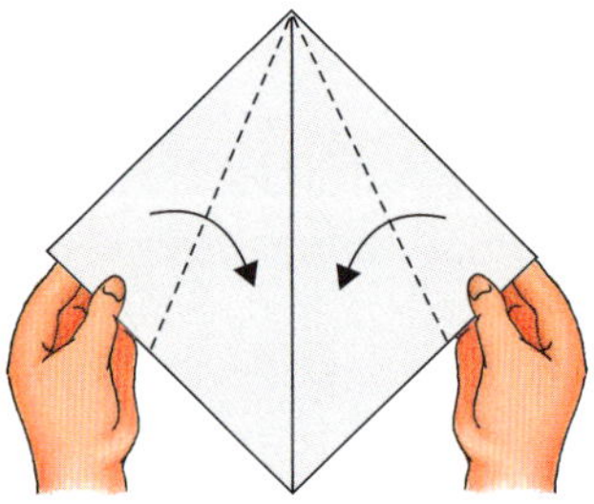

16 For making face, take another paper and fold it along the dotted lines.

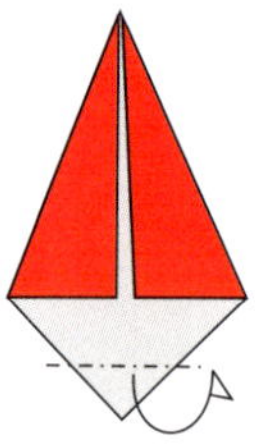

17 Fold the lower tip backward as shown.

18 Draw eyes, nose and lips on the face and paste it over the body, and your Joker is ready.

Jumping Frog

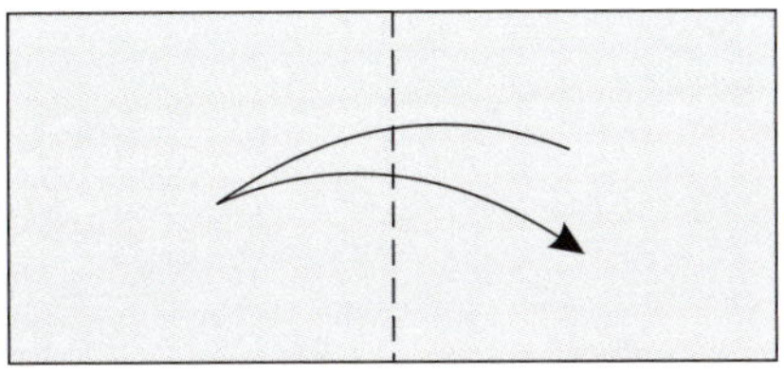

1 Take half sheet of the paper. Make a centre crease and then unfold.

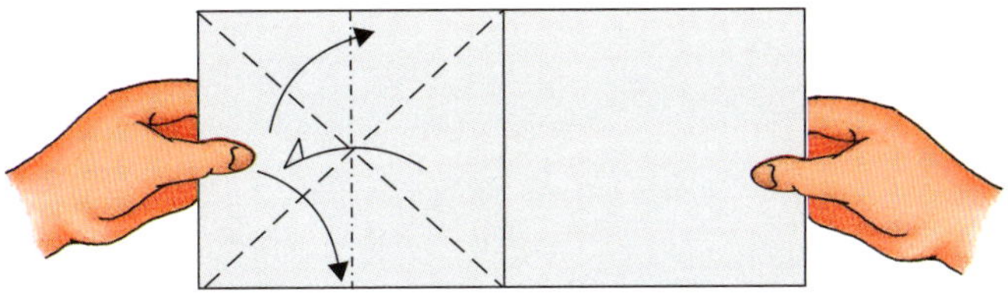

2 Make all the three folds on the left side in the direction of arrows, and then unfold.

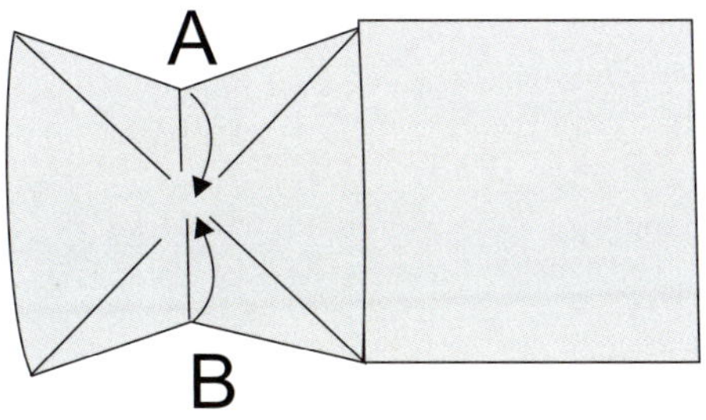

3 Make points 'A' and 'B' touch each other by folding the paper in the direction of arrows.

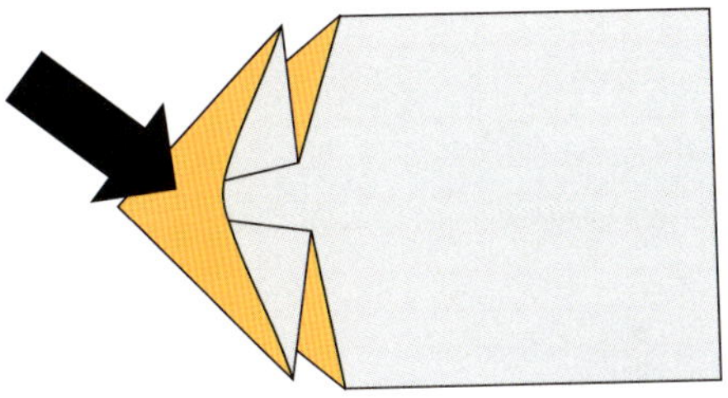

4 Now press the top triangular flap to flatten it.

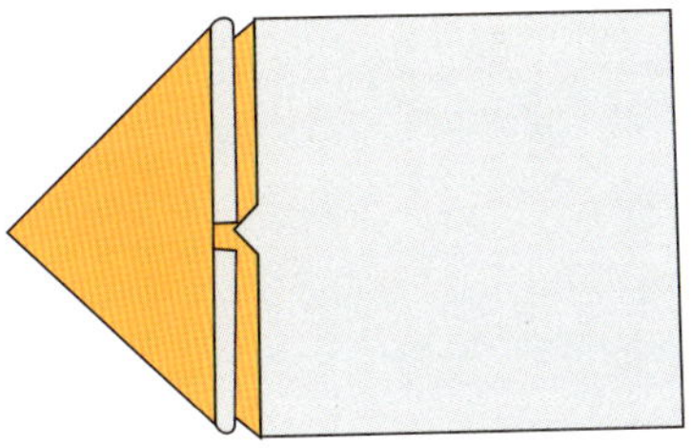

5 Your form will look like this. Fold the right side in the same way.

6 Fold all the four flaps along the dotted lines.

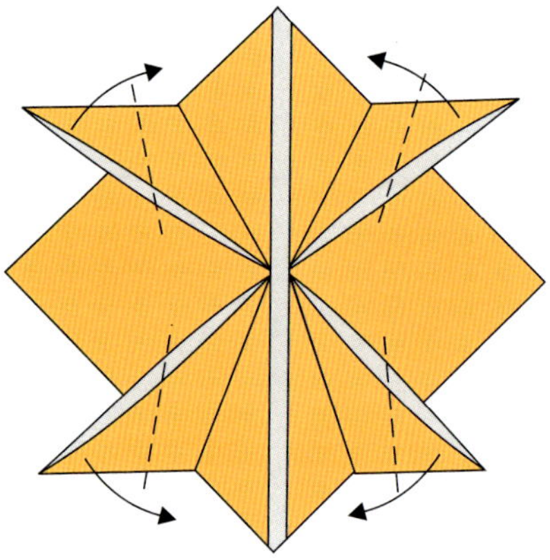

7 Again fold all the four flaps in the direction of arrows.

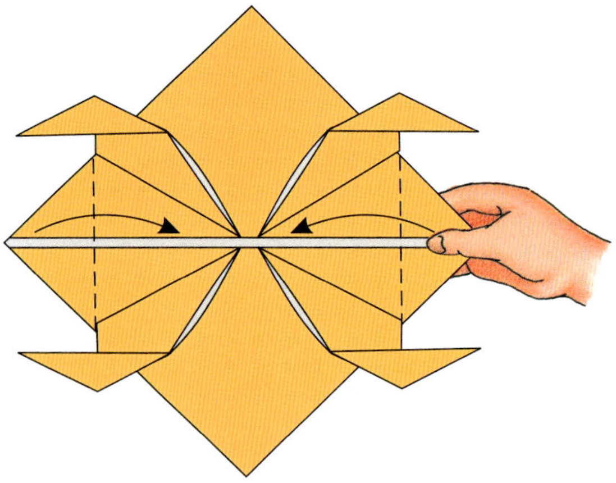

8 Change the direction of the form and make folds as shown.

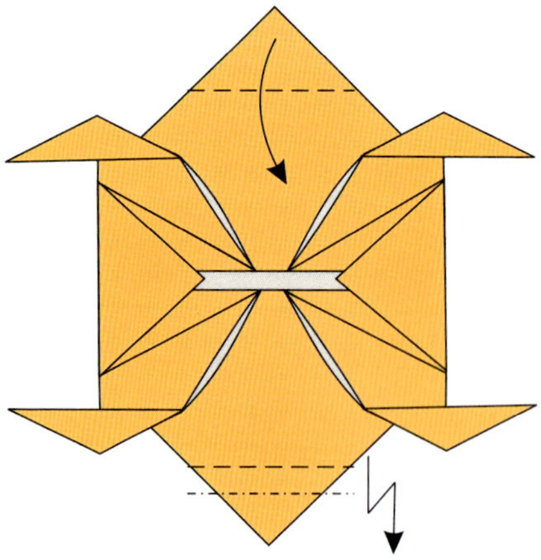

9 Make a valley fold at the top and stair-step fold at the bottom as shown.

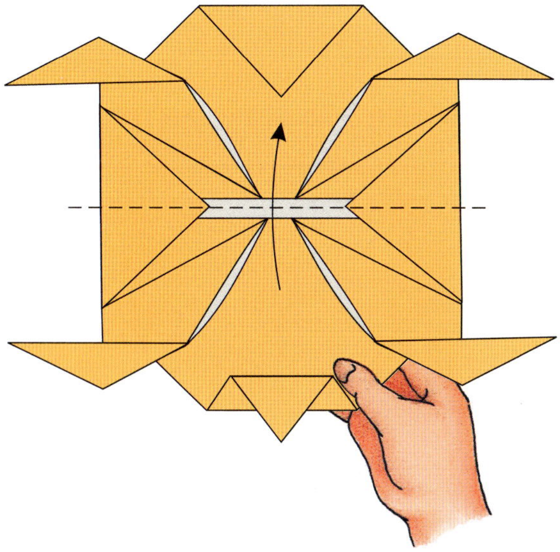

10 Fold the form in half along the dotted line.

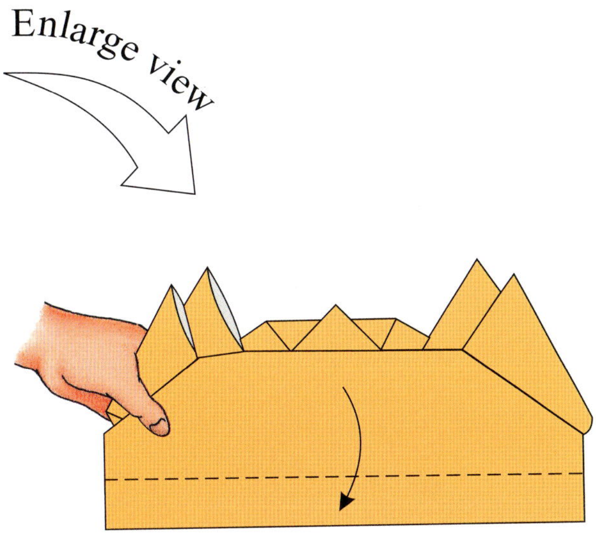

11 Fold the upper flap downward along the dotted line in the direction of arrow.

12 Your form will look like this.

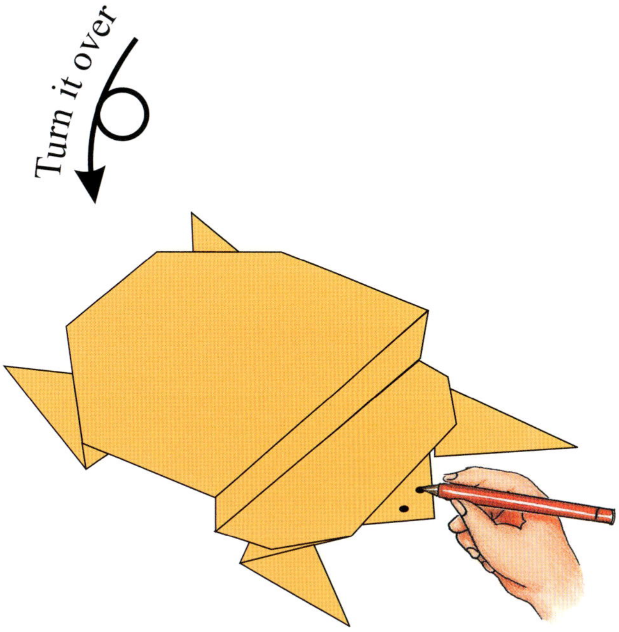

13 Draw eyes, and your frog is ready to jump if you press its back gently.

Horse

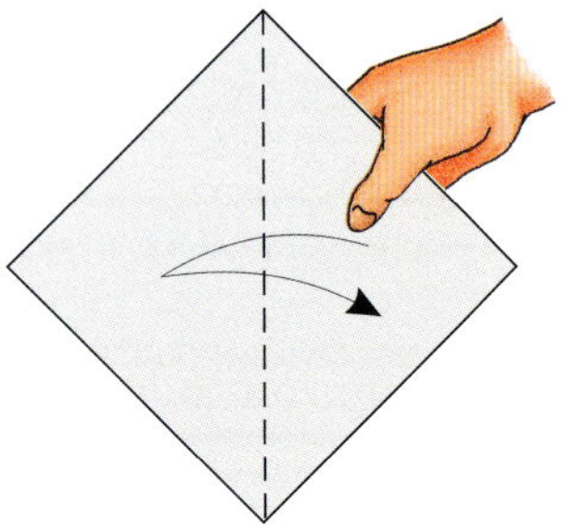

1 Fold the paper in half and unfold.

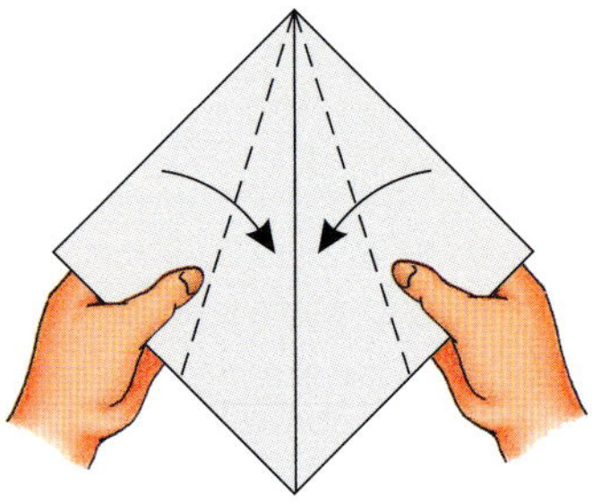

2 Fold the right and left sides to the centre crease.

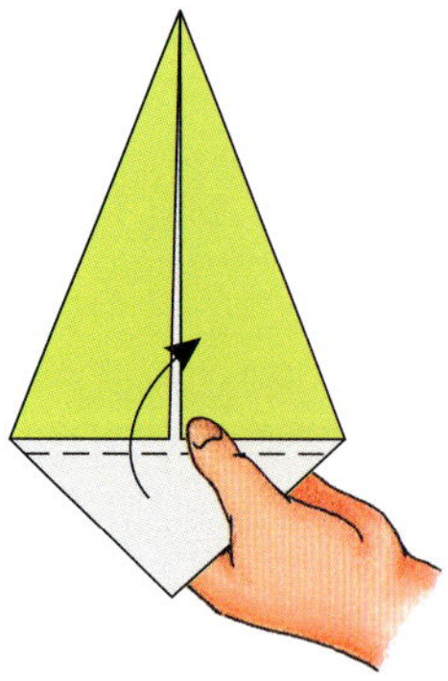

3 Fold the lower end upward and tuck it under both the flaps.

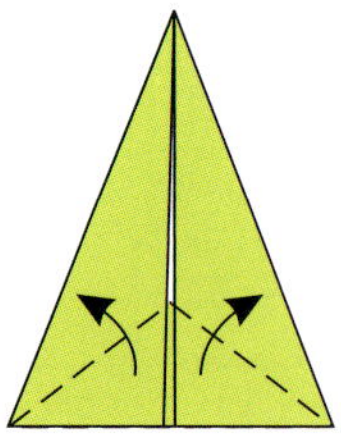

4 Fold both the flaps upward along the dotted lines.

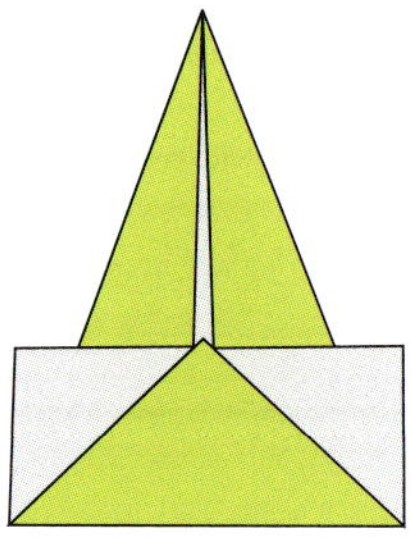

5 Your form will look like this.

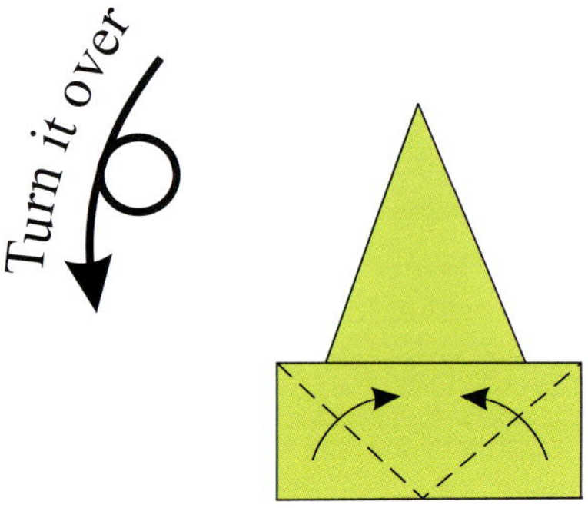

6 Now fold both lower corners upwards along the dotted lines.

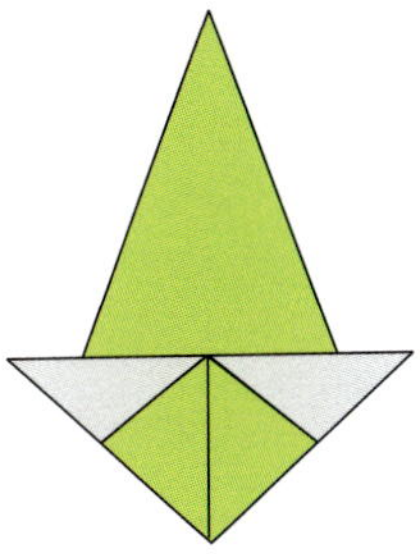

7 Your form will look like this.

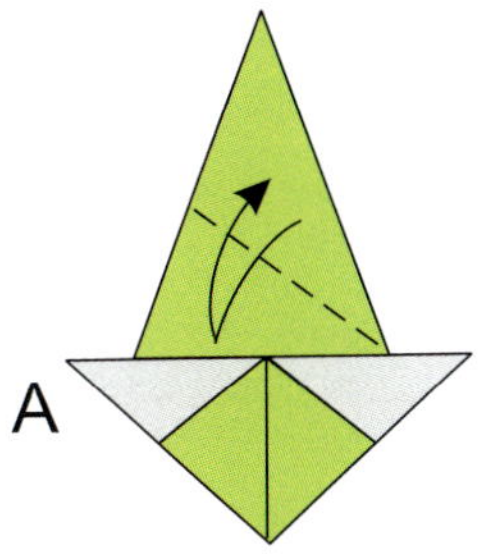

8 Fold the tip of the form downwards to meet the point 'A'. Make crease and unfold it.

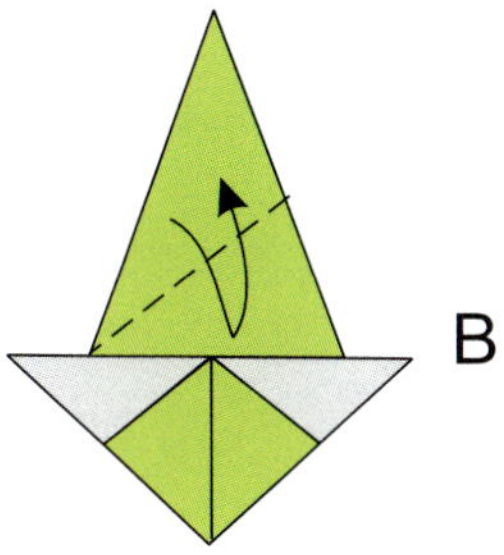

9 Fold the tip of the form downwards to meet the point 'B'. Make crease and unfold it.

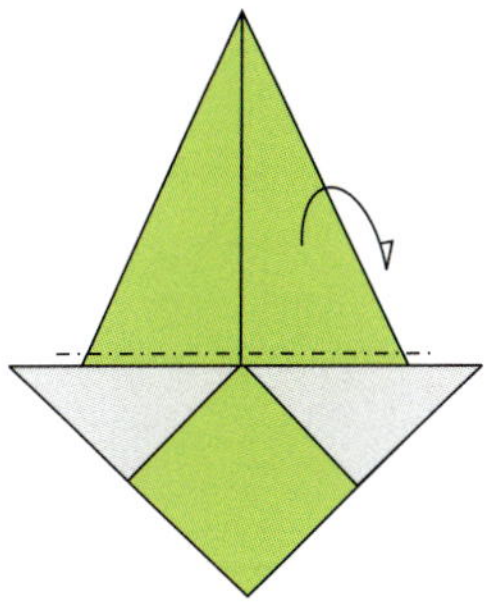

10 Now, make a mountain fold along the dotted line. The top point will go beyond the bottom point of the form.

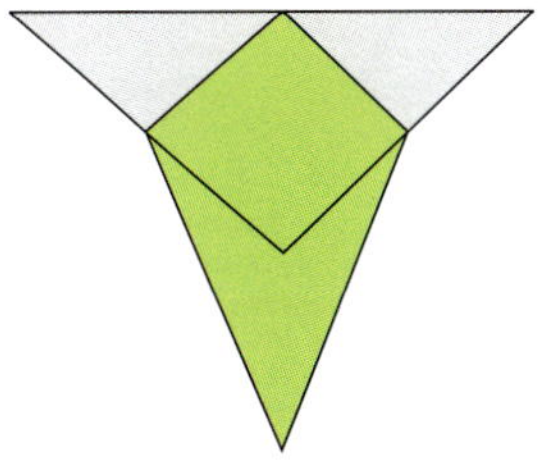

11 Your form will look like this. Now, unfold it after making a sharp crease along the folded line.

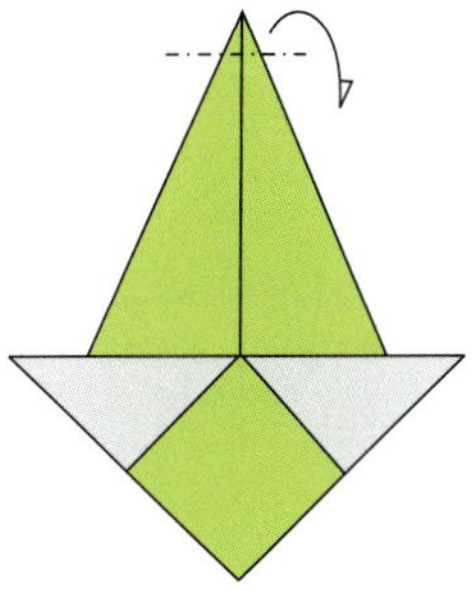

12 Now fold the top portion backward, using a mountain fold, along the dotted line.

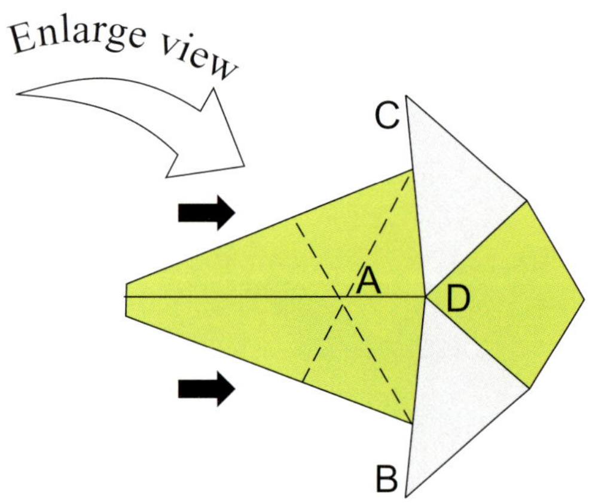

13 Now follow these steps carefully. Put the form in your hands as shown. Use your thumb and forefinger of the left hand and push the form a little inside. The left portion will automatically get folded inside at point 'A'....

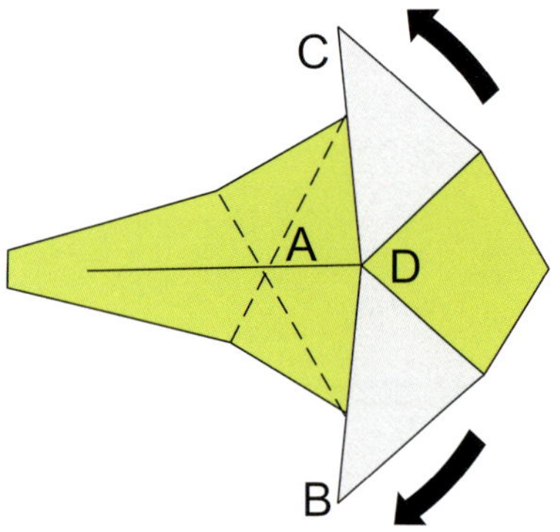

14 ....at the same time, fold the form in half so that the corners 'B' and 'C'meet each other.

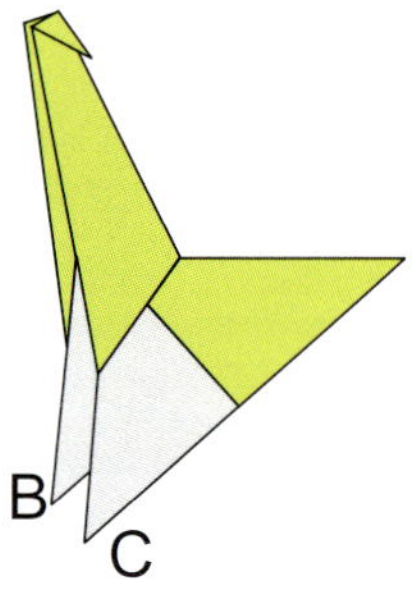

15 Try all the steps until your form looks like this. The horse neck automatically pops up.

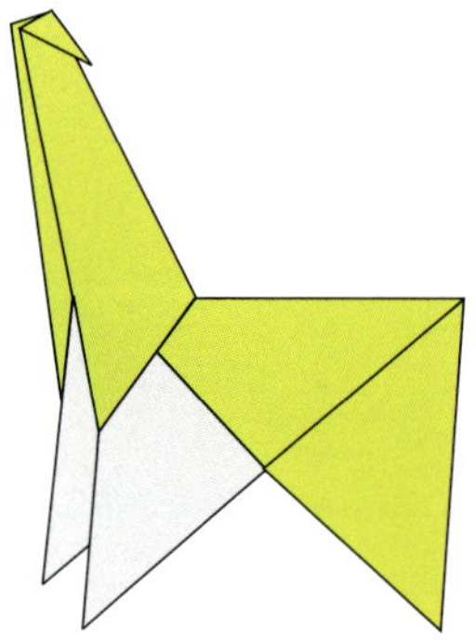

16 For the back legs of the horse, slightly open the form from below and pick out the point 'D' downwards (for position of point 'D' see figures no. 13 and 14). The form will take its shape automatically thereafter.

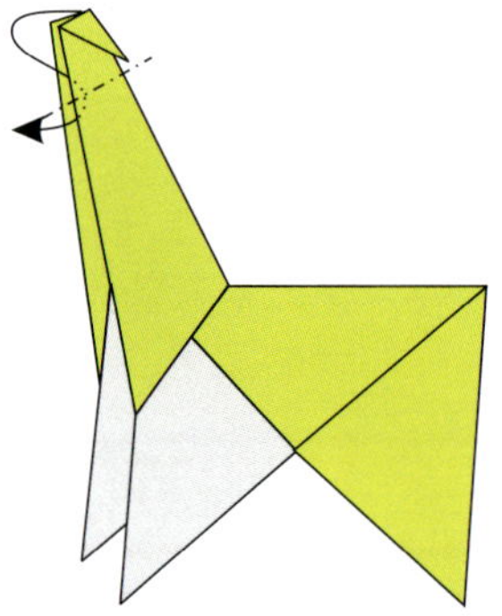

17 For head of the horse, make a pocket fold along the dotted line in the direction of arrow.

18 Now draw and decorate your horse and paste paper stripes to form its tail.

Collage Work

Yacht

TIPS AND TRICKS

Step-1 Collect paper sheets of various colours of your own choice. Tear them in small pieces of different shapes.

Step-2 Set them within the outline and paste in the given shape.

Cut and Paste

Rooster

TIPS AND TRICKS

Step-1 Take craft paper sheets of various colours. Trace different parts on the shape of different colours.

Step-2 Now paste these pieces at the appropriate places.

Crushed Paper Art

Joker

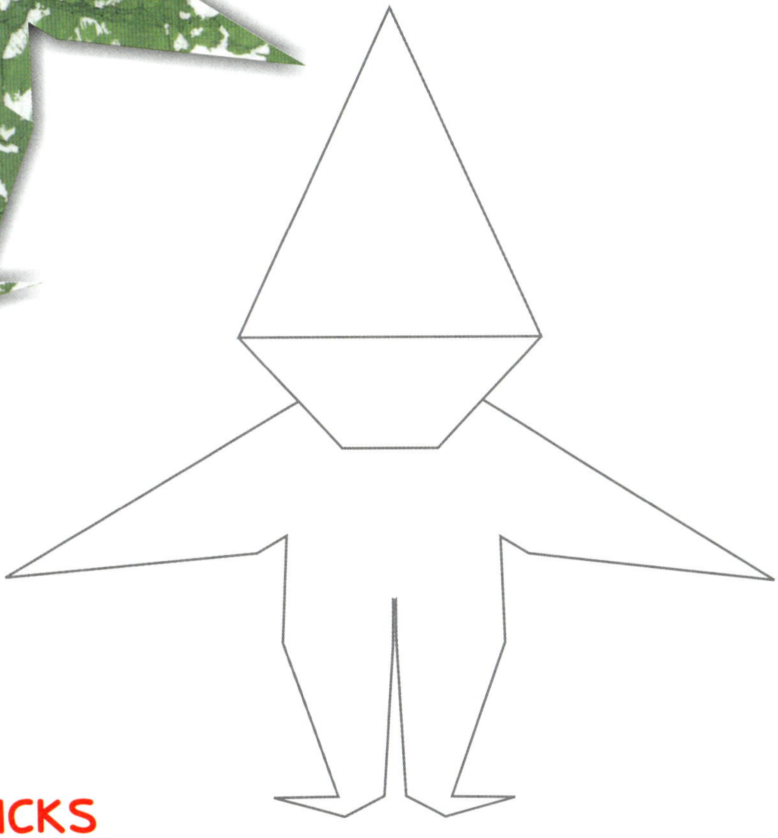

TIPS AND TRICKS

Step-1 Take a plain paper and squeeze it in your hand. Open it gently and apply the poster colour with a flat brush.

Step-2 Now cut the paper according to the shape and paste it within the outline.

Spray Paint

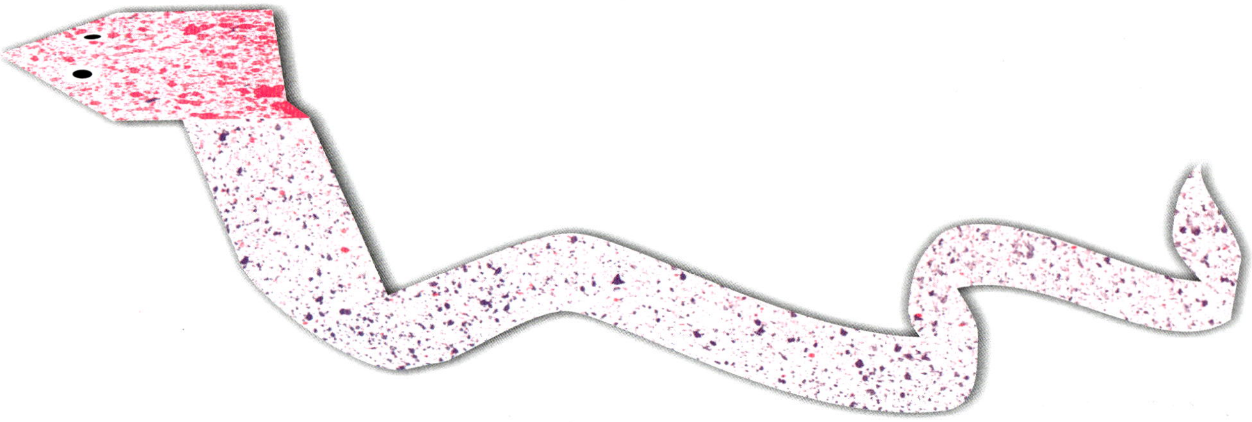

King Cobra

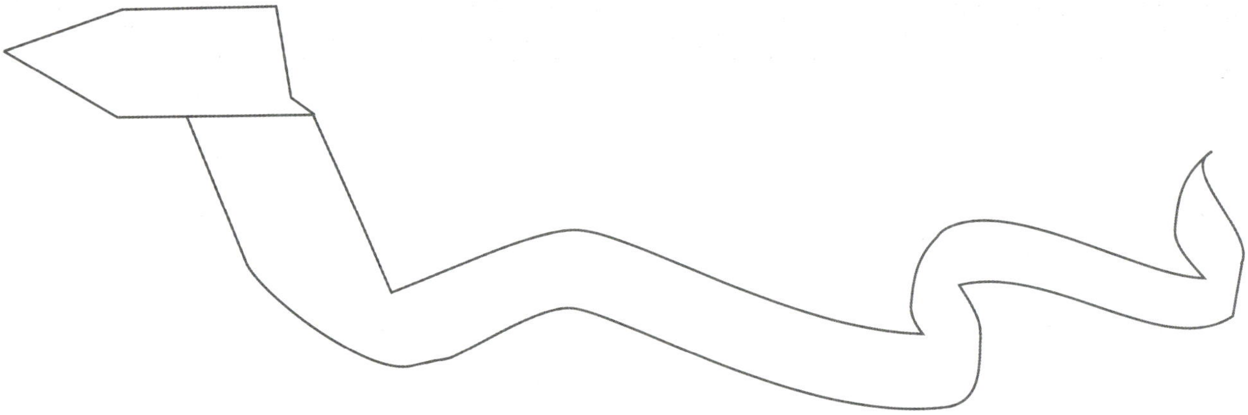

TIPS AND TRICKS

Step-1 Take a white paper. Spray different colours of your own choice with a tooth brush on the white paper.

Step-2 Cut the parts of the shape as per your liking and paste them on the figure.

Fox

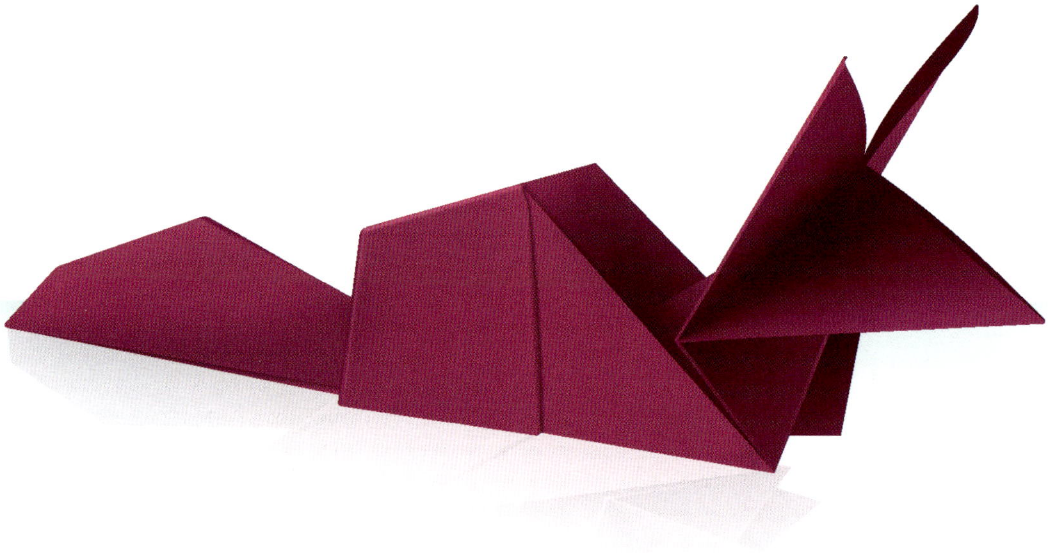

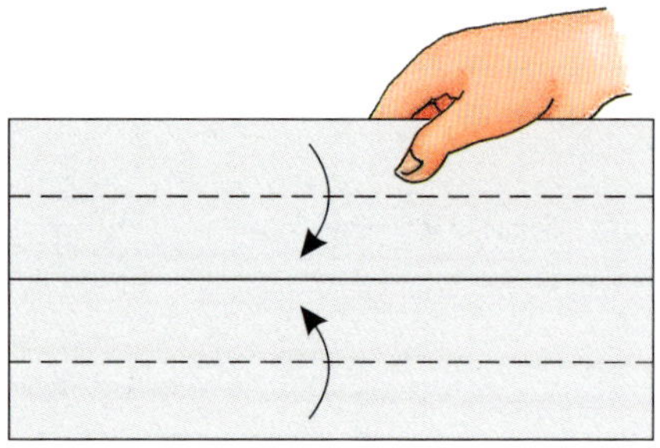

1 Take a rectangular paper and fold inside along the dotted lines.

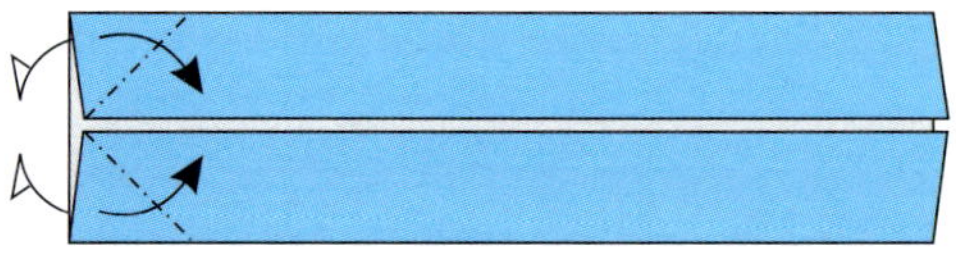

2 Make forward and backward folds along the dotted lines. Unfold them and tuck both the corners inside....

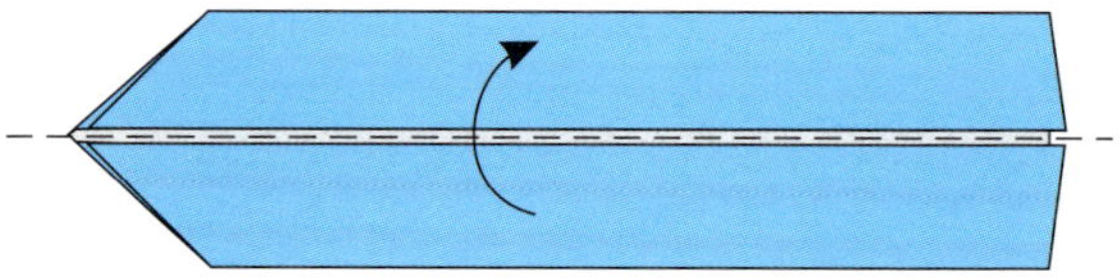

3 .... like this. Fold the form in half along the dotted line.

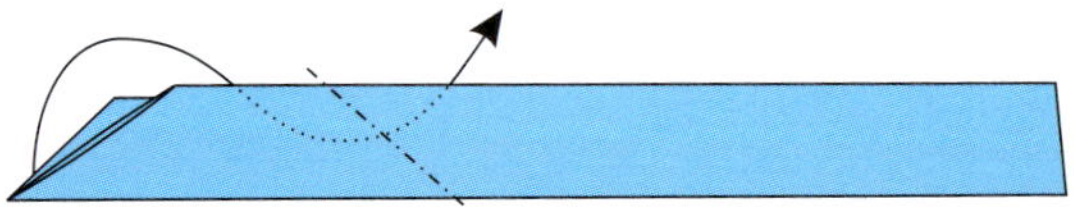

4 Fold the left side along the dotted line upwards, using the pocket fold.

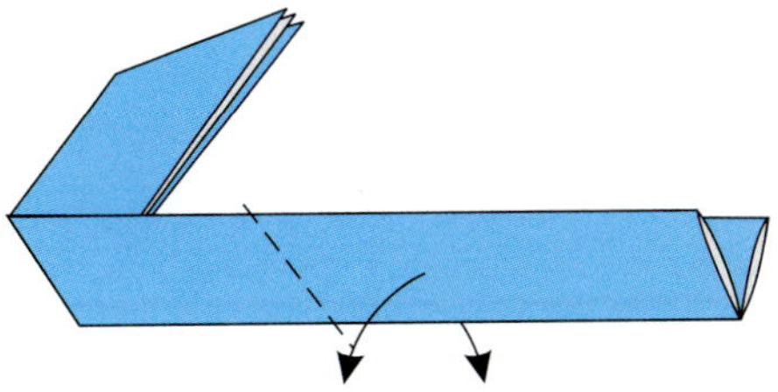

5 Make a hood fold along the dotted line.

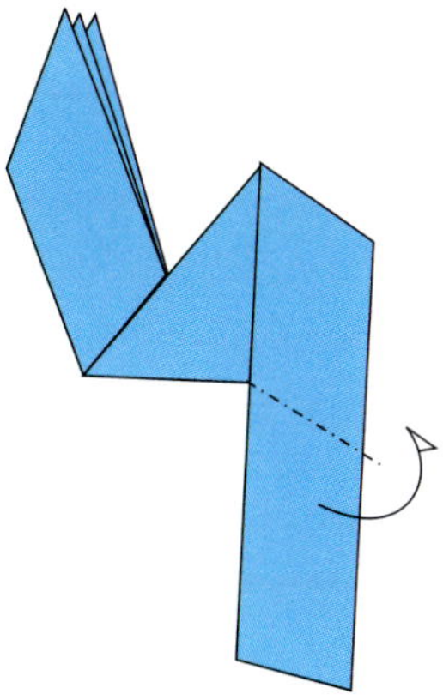

6 Fold backward along the dotted line.

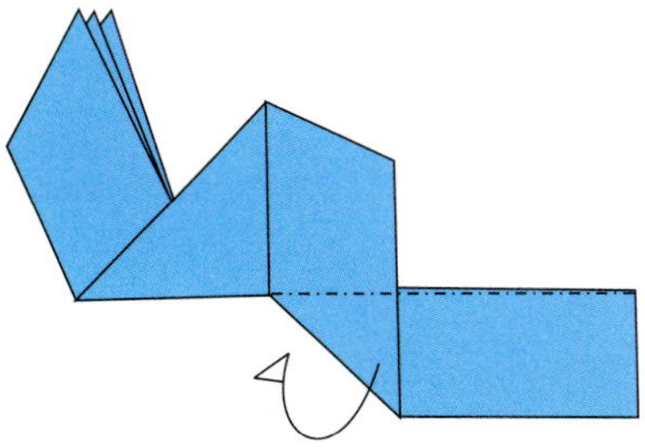

7 Fold the bottom part upward behind the form along the dotted line.

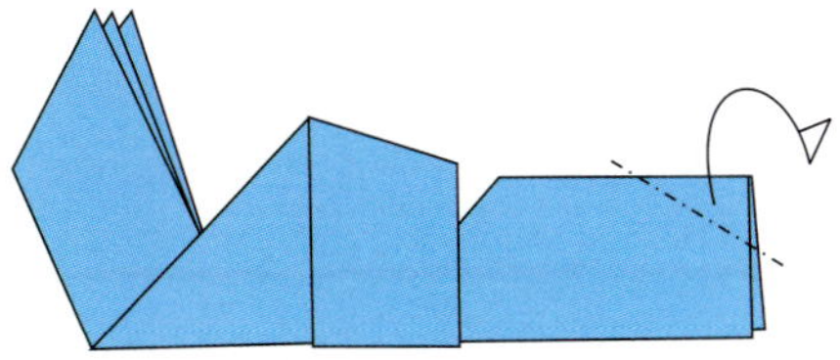

8 Now fold the top corner of the right flap backward along the dotted line.

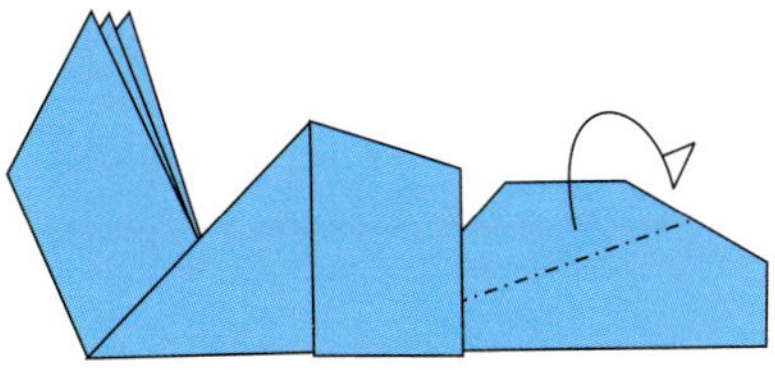

9 Again fold the right flap backward in the direction of arrow.

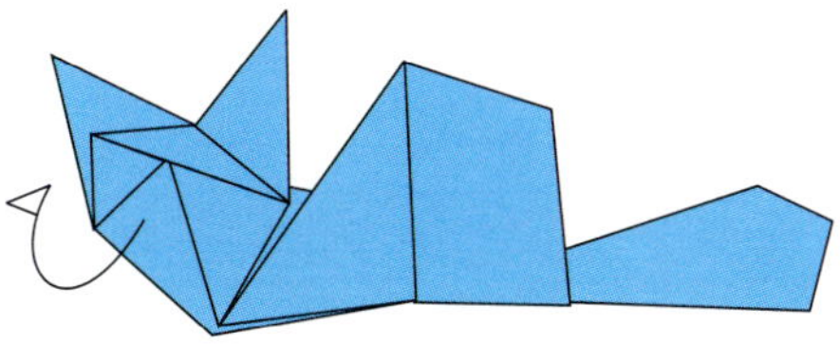

10 Now open left flap to make the face of the fox. Your fox is ready.

Peacock

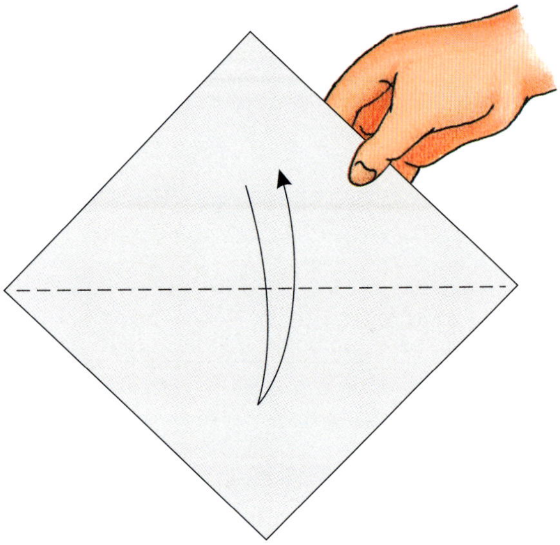

1 Fold the paper in half and unfold.

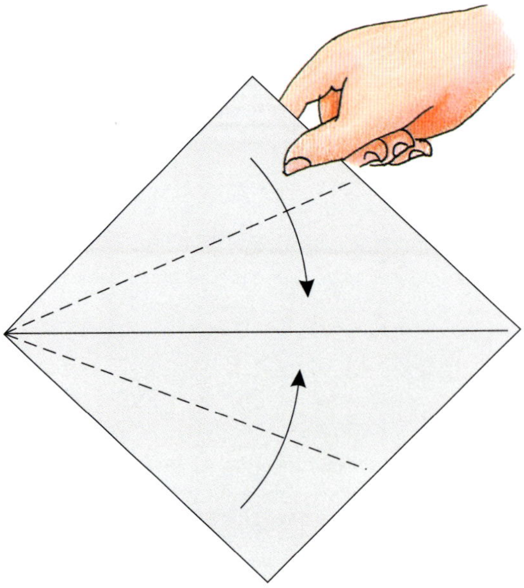

2 Fold the top and bottom corner to the centre line.

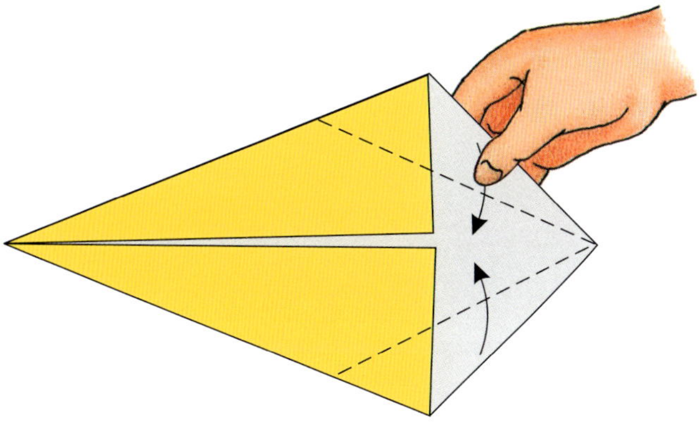

3 Fold the bottom and top corners inside along the dotted lines.

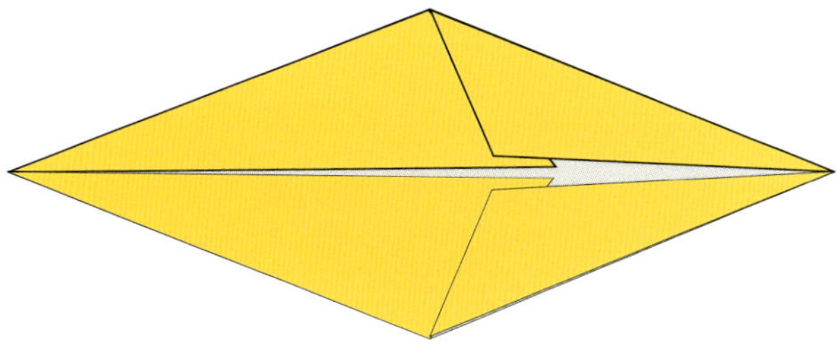

4 Your form will look like this.

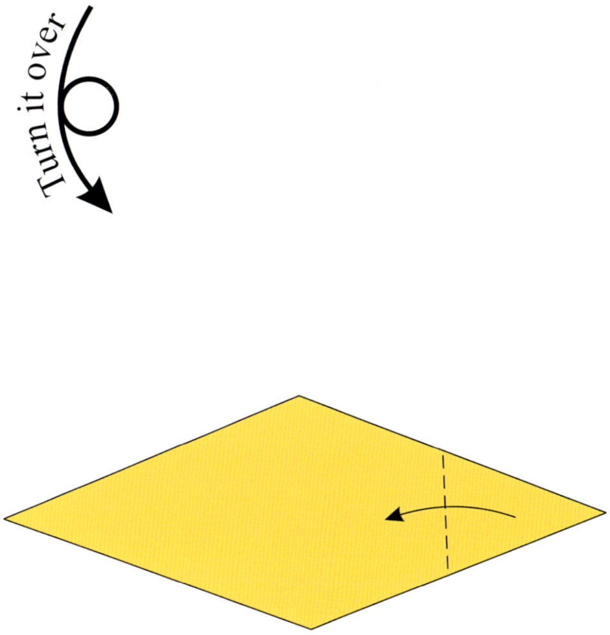

5 Fold the right corner inside along the dotted line.

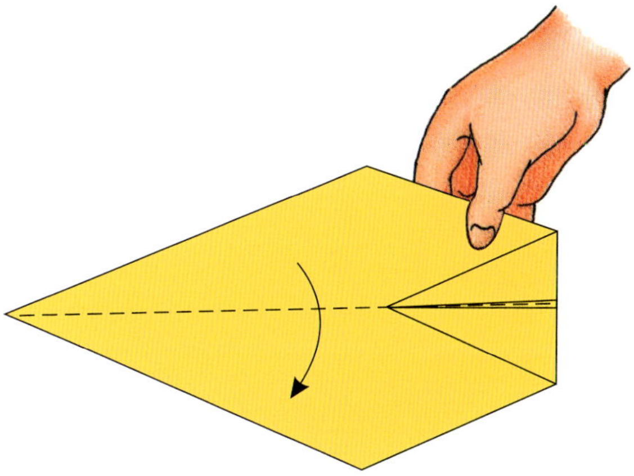

6 Make a valley fold along the dotted line.

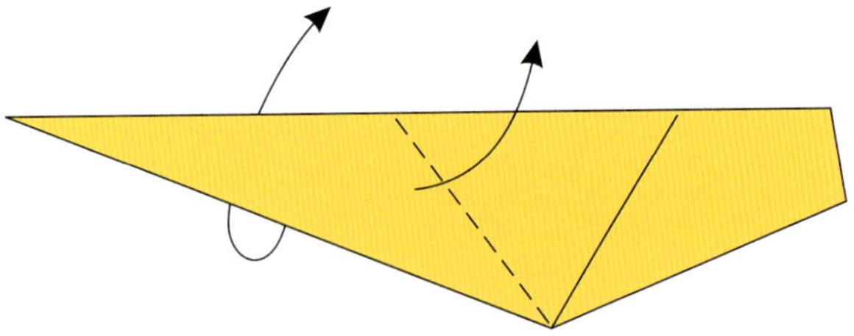

7 Make a hood fold along the dotted line....

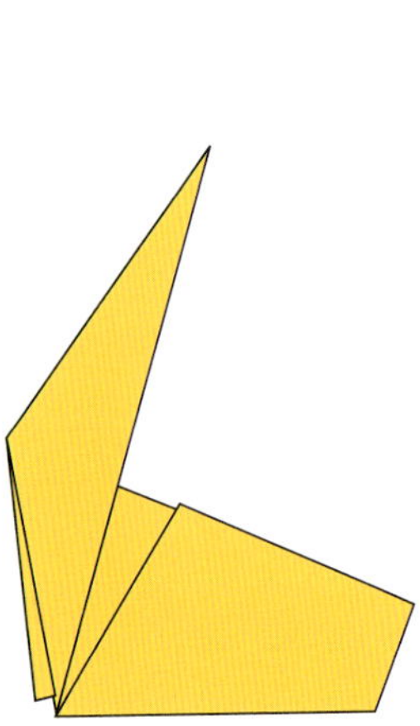

8 .... like this.

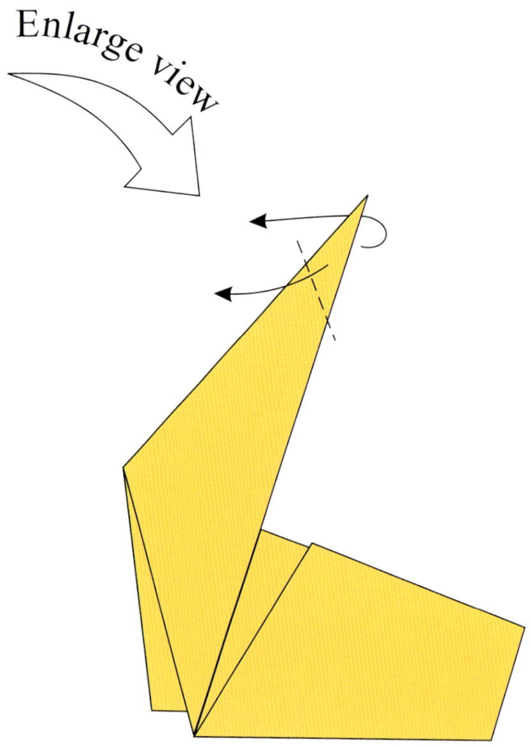

9 Again make a hood fold along the dotted line.

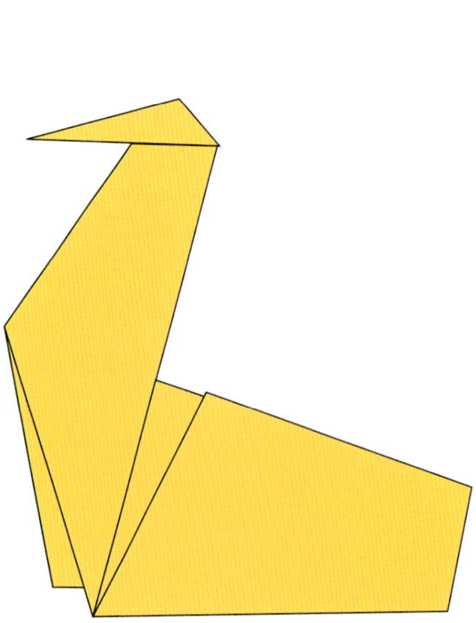

10 Now the body of peacock is ready.

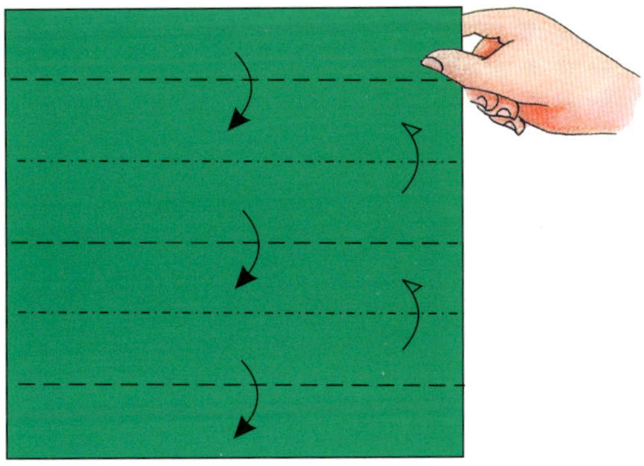

11 For making the feathers take another paper and start with valley and mountain folds alternately....

12 ....like this.

13 Fold another paper in the same way and put them in this manner.

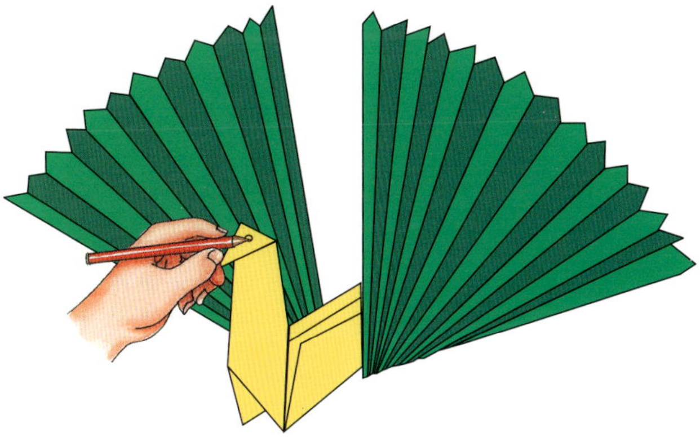

14 Draw eyes and paste the feathers at the back of the body. Now, your peacock is ready to dance.

Talking Crow

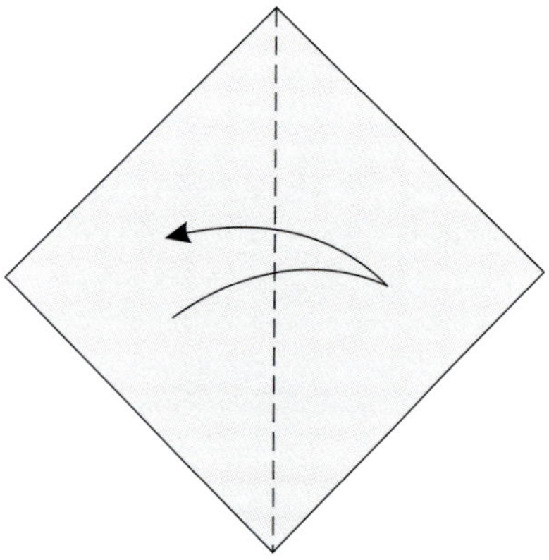

1 Fold in half to make a centre crease, then unfold.

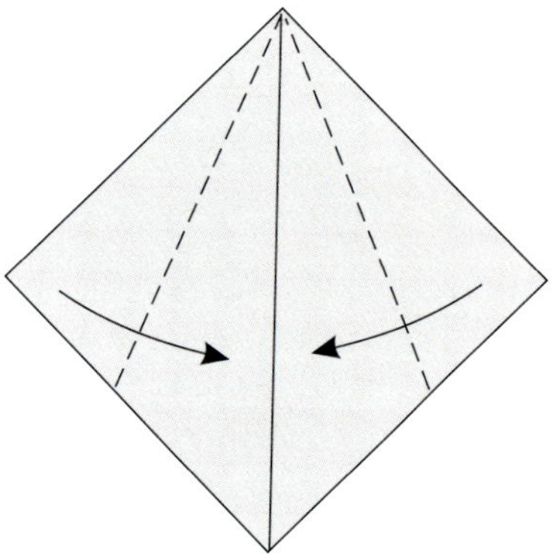

2 Make folds inside along the dotted lines.

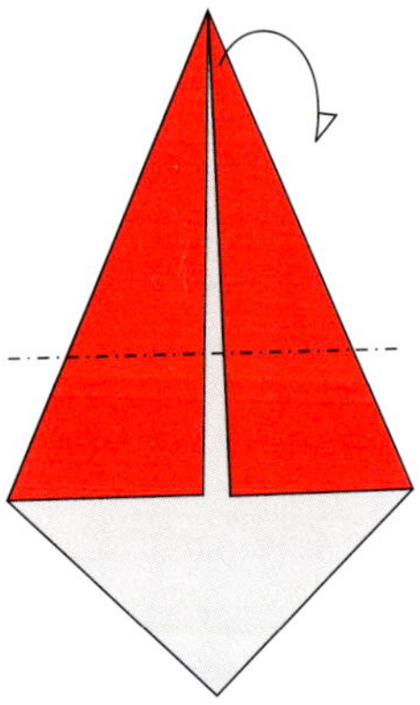

3 Fold the top corner backward to meet the bottom corner.

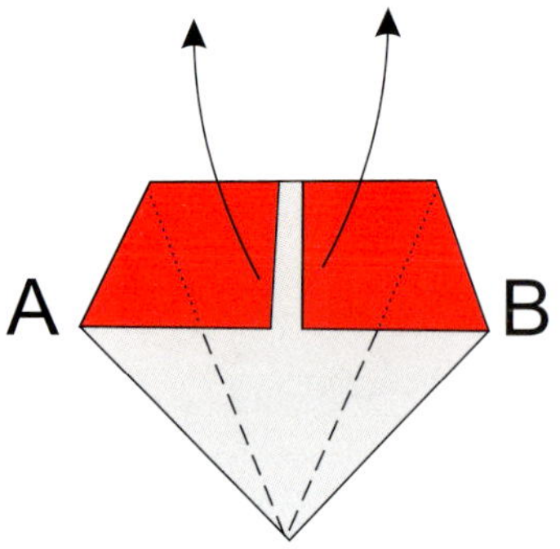

4 Fold and then unfold along the dotted lines. Now, pull both the top flaps up so the points 'A' and 'B' come to the centre line.

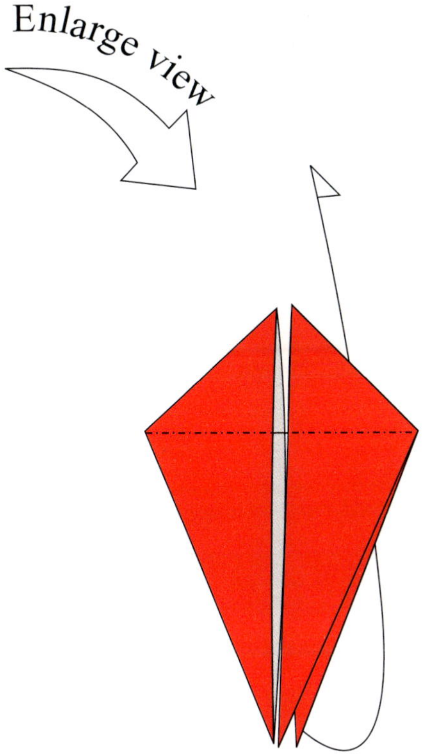

5 Now make the back flap up along the dotted line.

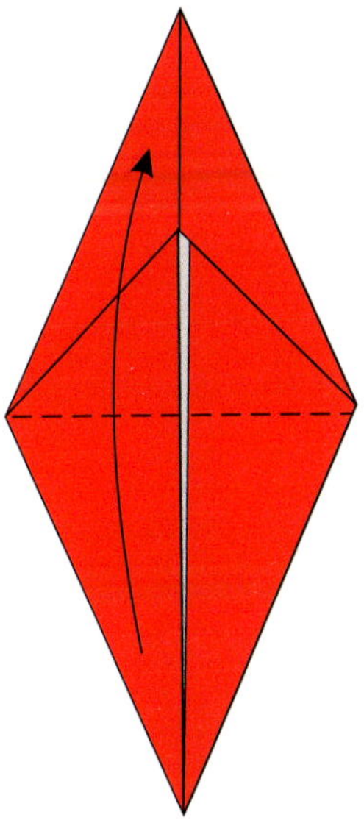

6 Fold the bottom corner upwards to meet the top corner.

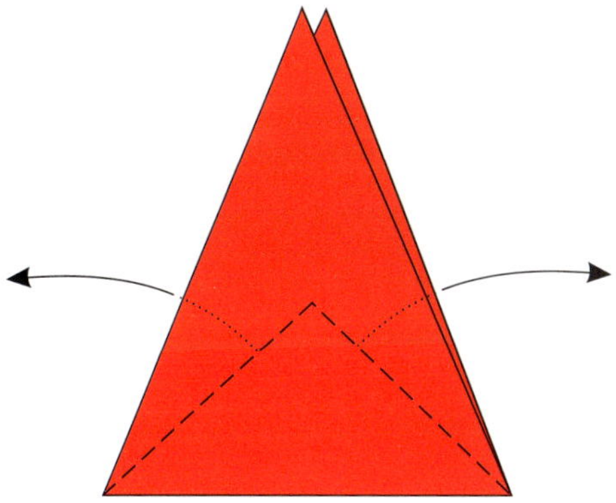

7 Pull both the hidden triangles outside as shown.

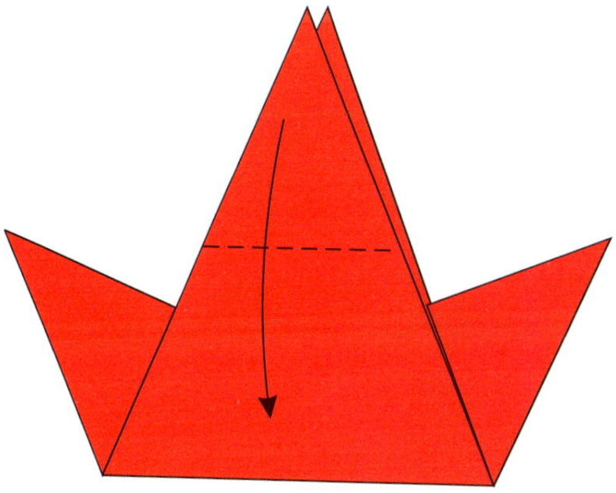

8 Fold the upper flap downwards.

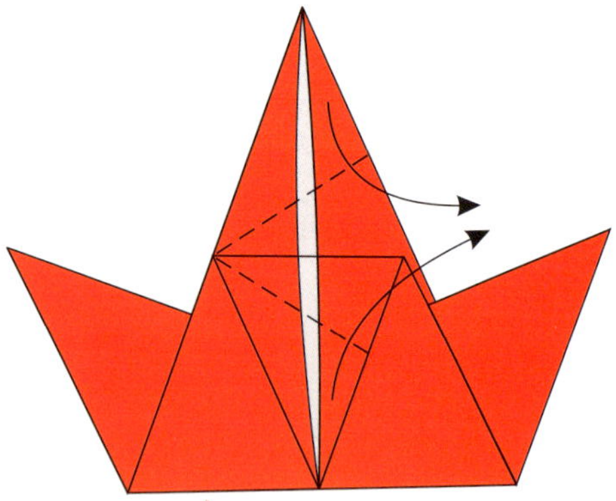

9 Fold along the dotted lines in the direction of arrows.

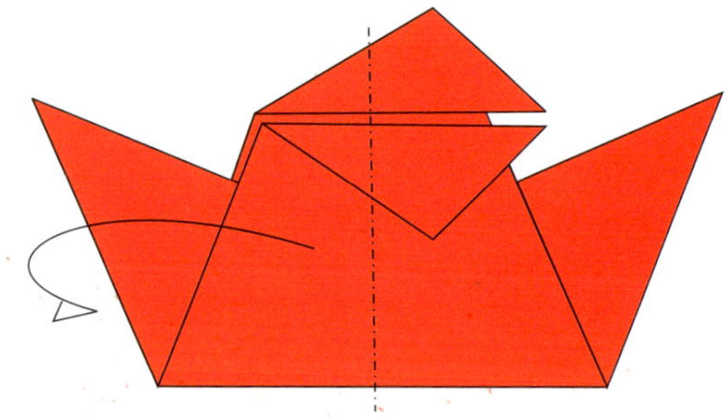

10 Fold the left portion backward along the dotted line

11 Now, open the upper flaps towards left and press it to make the beak.

12 Draw eyes and pull the back flaps apart. Your bird is ready to crow-crow.

Animal Head

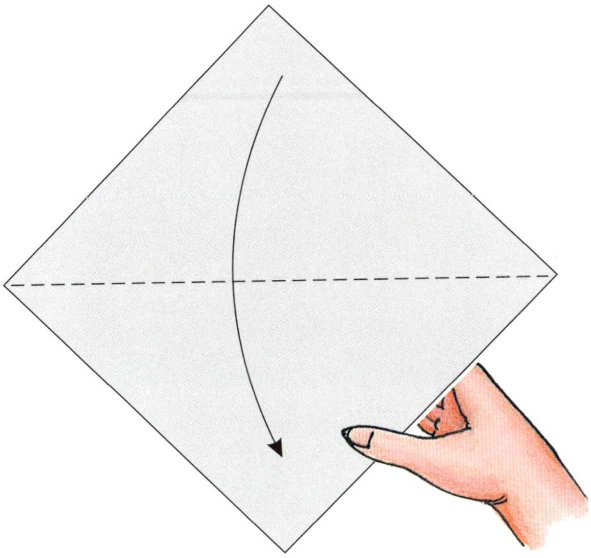

1 Fold in half.

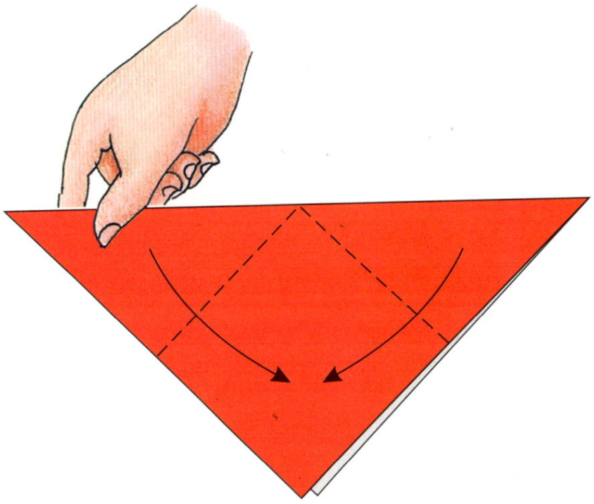

2 Fold the left and the right corners down to the lower end.

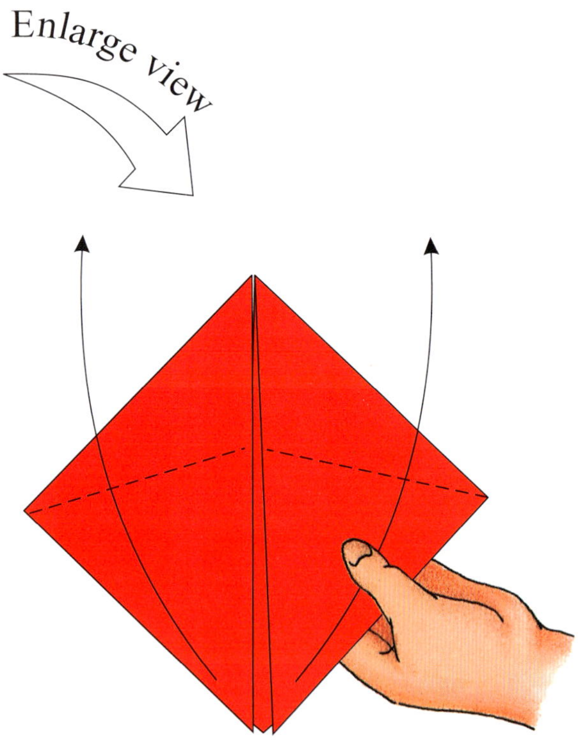

3 Fold both the flaps of the upper layer upwards as shown.

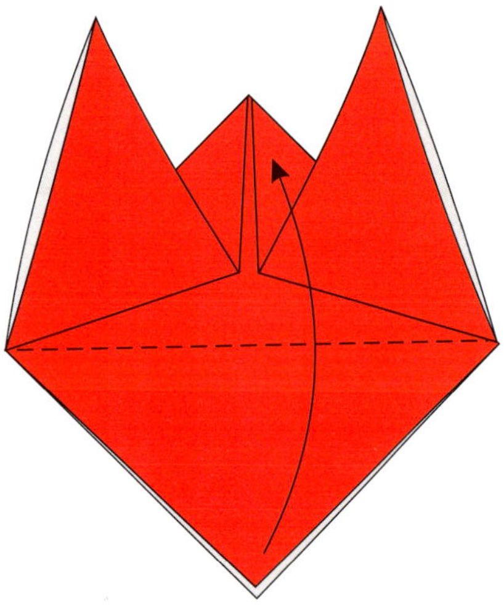

4 Fold the lower facing flap upwards....

5 .... like this.

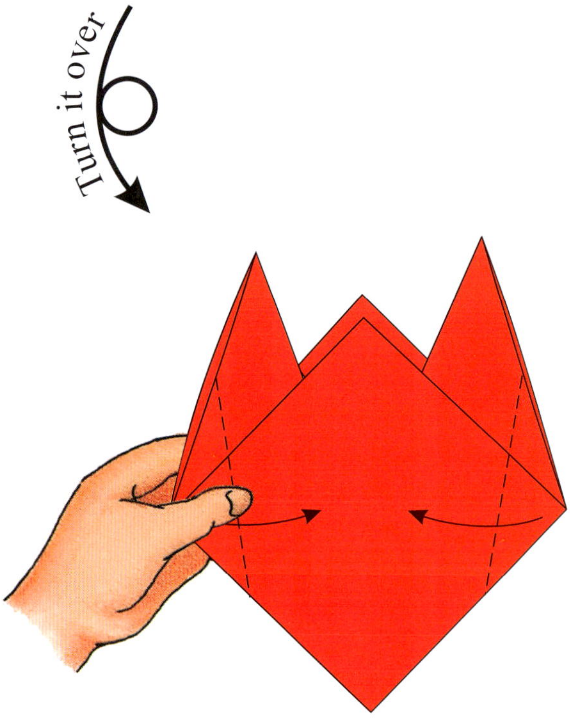

6 Now, fold the left and the right corners as shown.

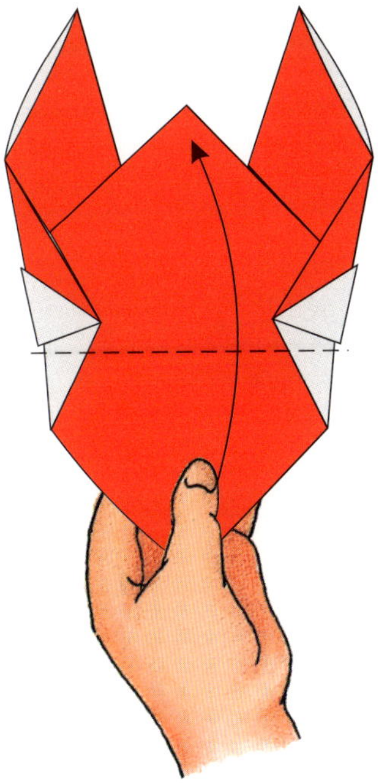

7 Fold the lower triangle along the direction of arrow.

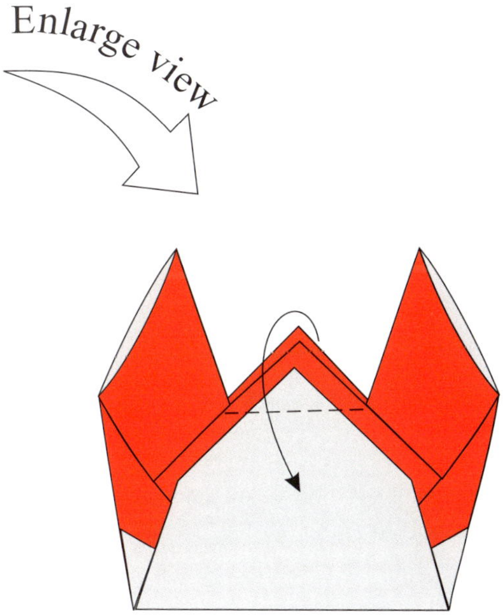

8 Fold the upper tips downwards.

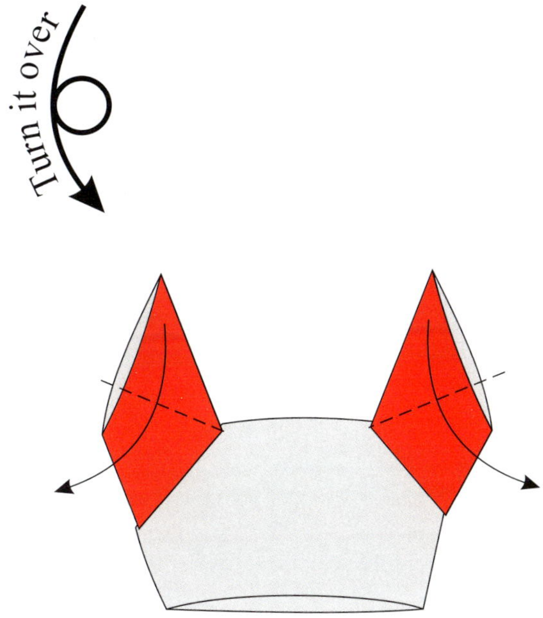

9 To make the doggie's ears, fold the top corners of flaps downwards as shown.

10 Draw face of the doggie, and your finger puppet is ready.

Ladybird

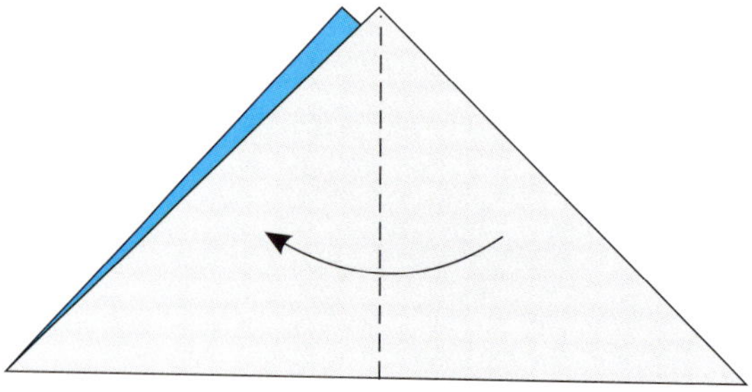

2 Again fold in the direction of arrow.

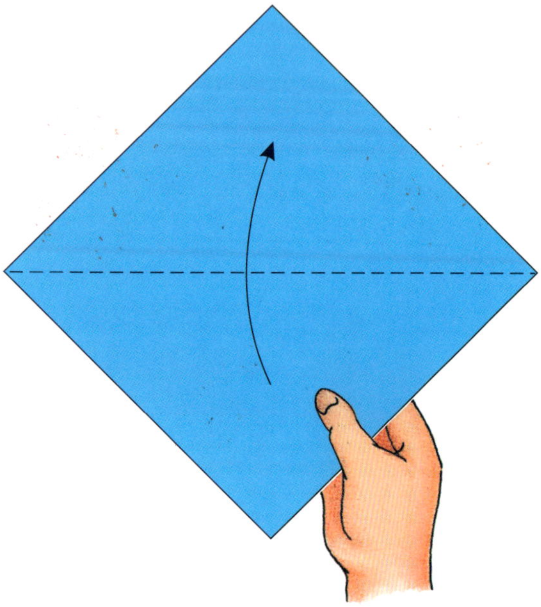

1 Fold in half.

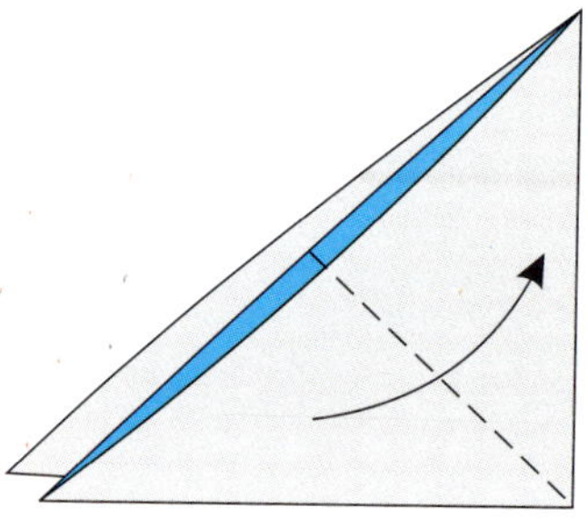

3 Open the front flap as shown.

4 Your form will look like this. Now, turn it over and fold in the same way.

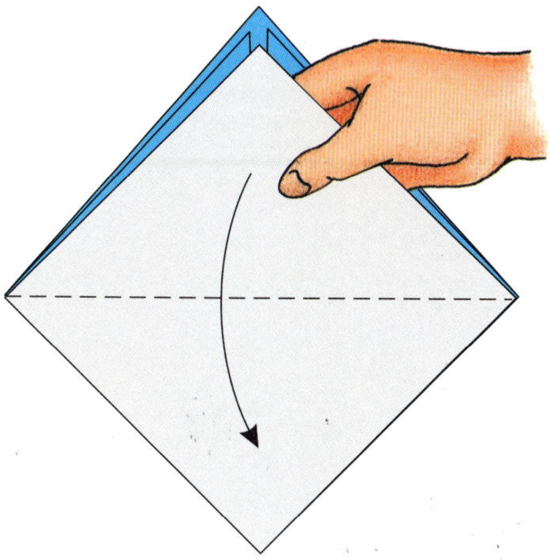

5 Your form will be like this. Fold the upper side of the top flap downward.

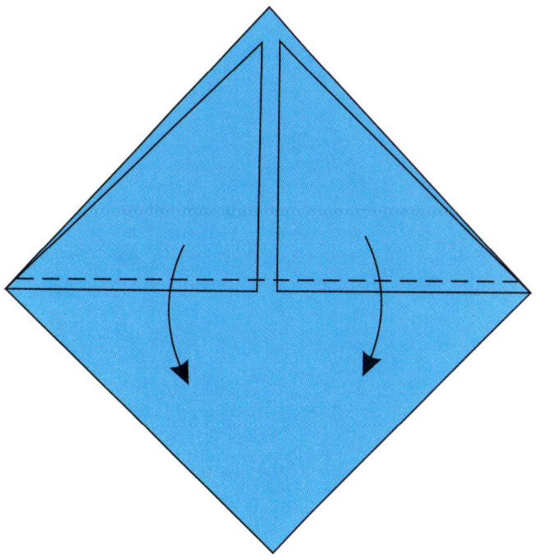

6 Bring both the triangular flaps down.

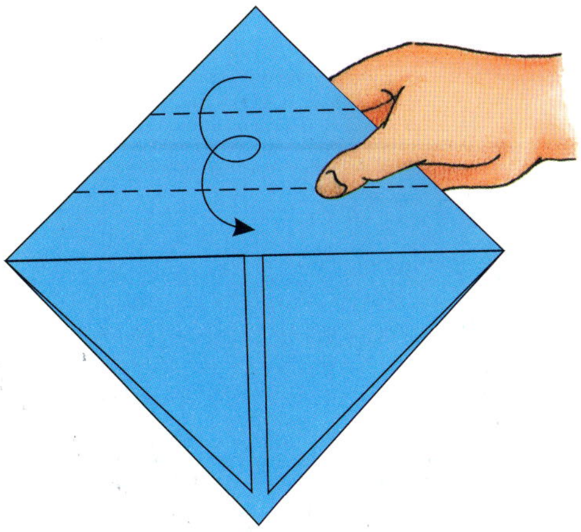

7 Fold twice along the dotted lines.

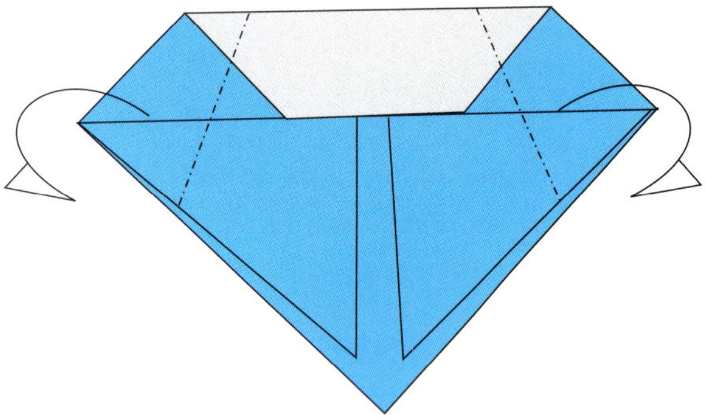

8 Fold both the side corners behind.

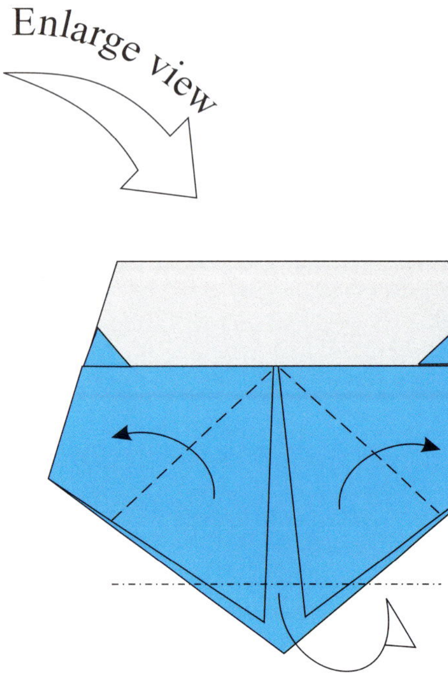

9 Fold and then unfold both the flaps. Fold the tail-end backward along the dotted line.

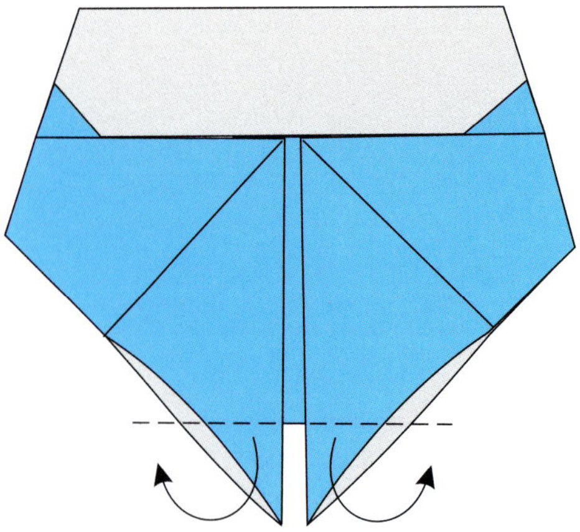

10 Fold both the lower corners inside along the dotted lines.

11 Draw black spots and eyes.

Balloon

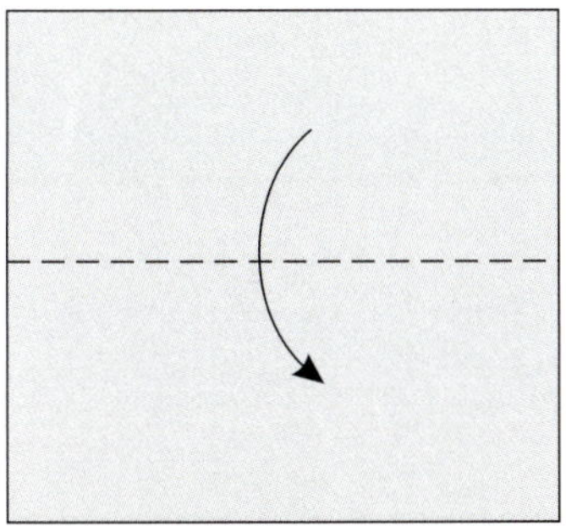

1 Fold the paper in half.

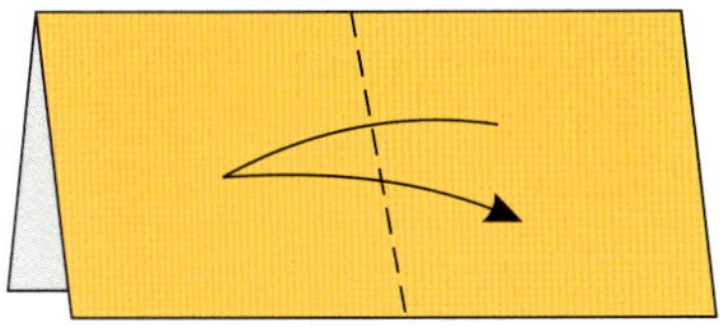

2 Fold in the direction of arrow, then unfold.

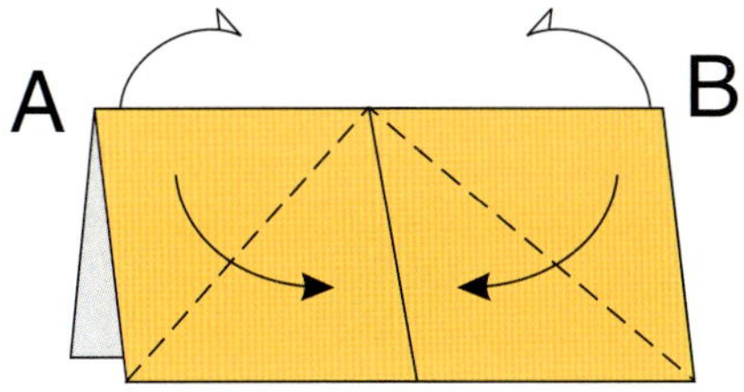

3 Fold points ‘A’ and ‘B’ forward and then backward along the dotted lines to make the creases.

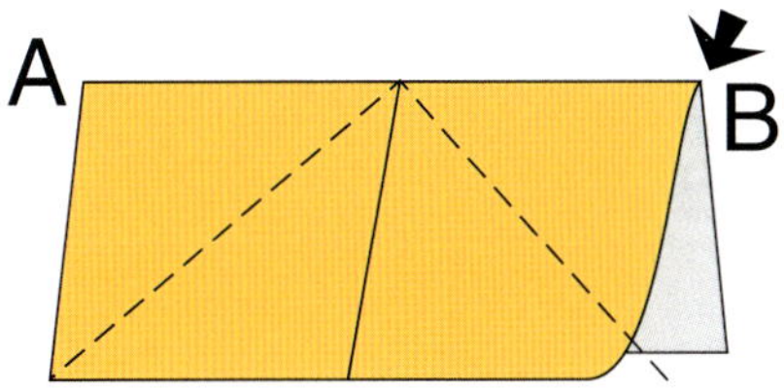

4 Open the form slightly and push point ‘B’ inside the form.

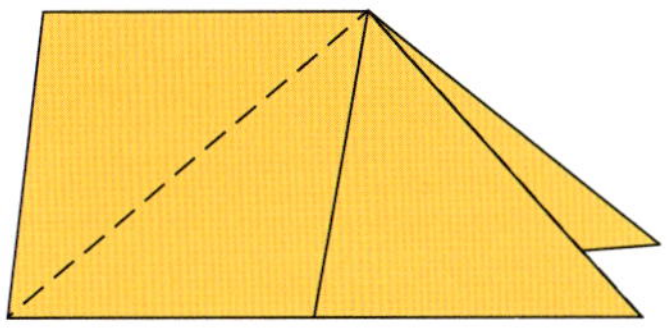

5 Your form will look like this.

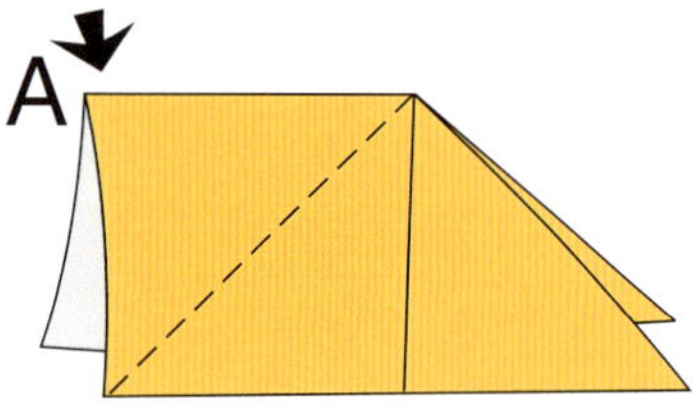

6 Now, push the point 'A' inside the form too, in the same way.

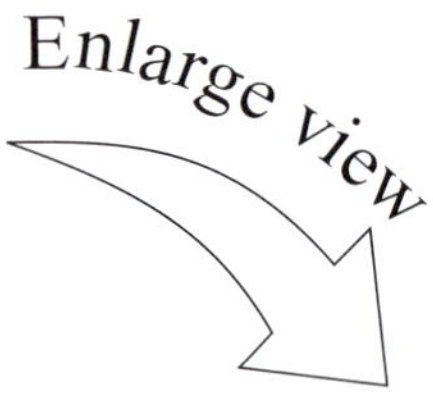

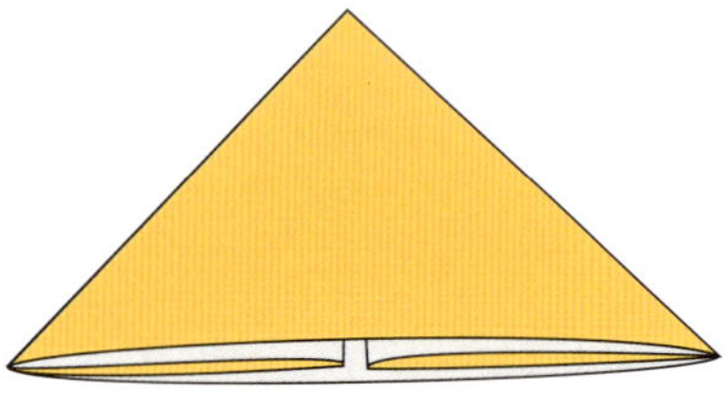

7 Your form will look like this.

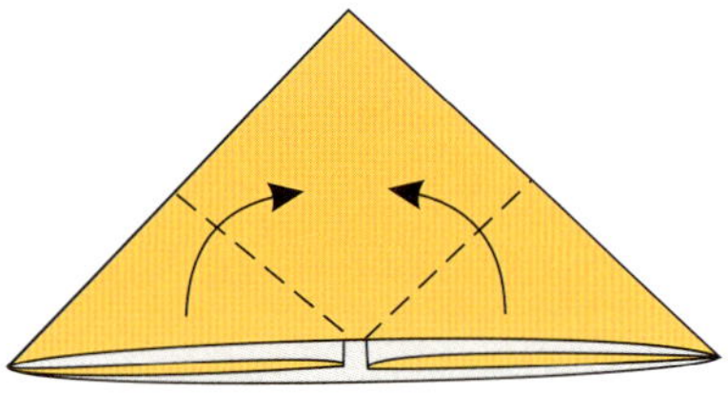

8 Now, fold the right and the left upper flaps upward along the dotted lines.

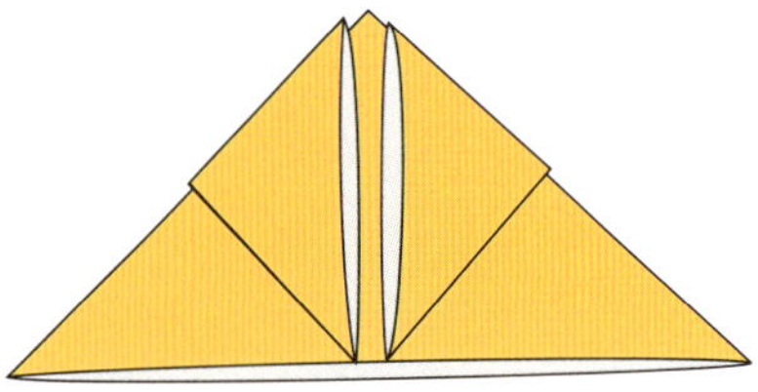

9 Your form will look like this.

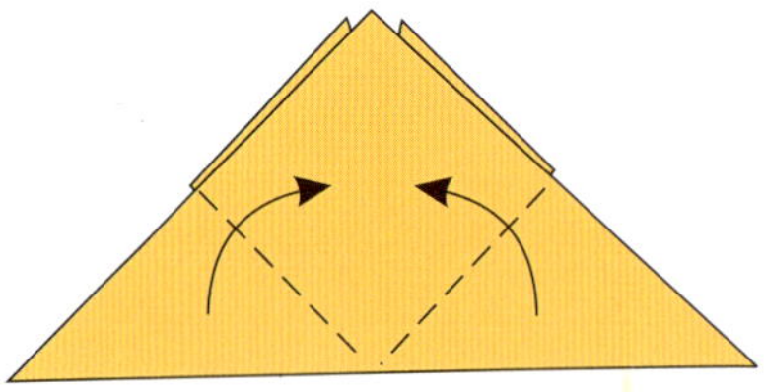

10 Again fold the right and the left flaps upward along the dotted lines.

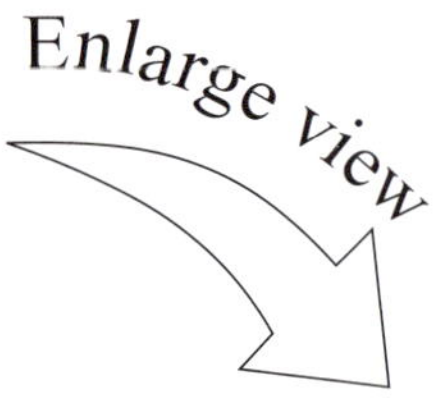

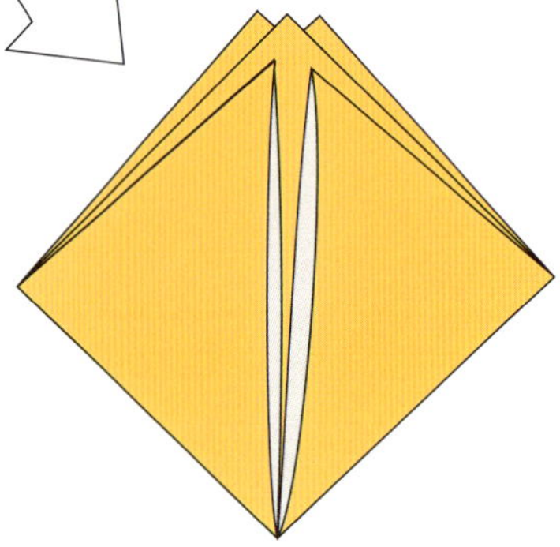

11 Your form will look like this.

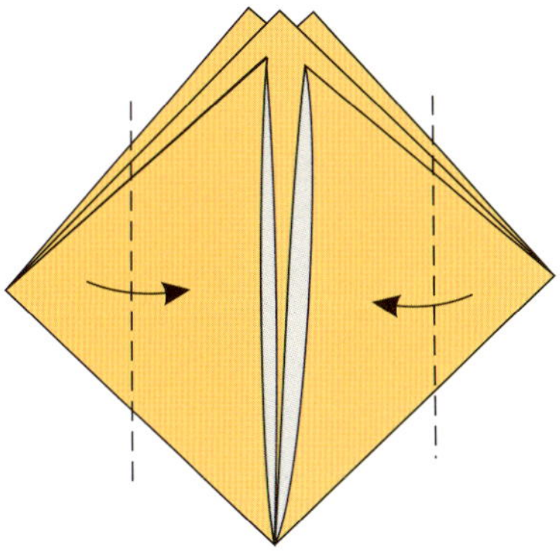

12 Now, fold both the right and the left corners of the upper flap inside along the dotted lines....

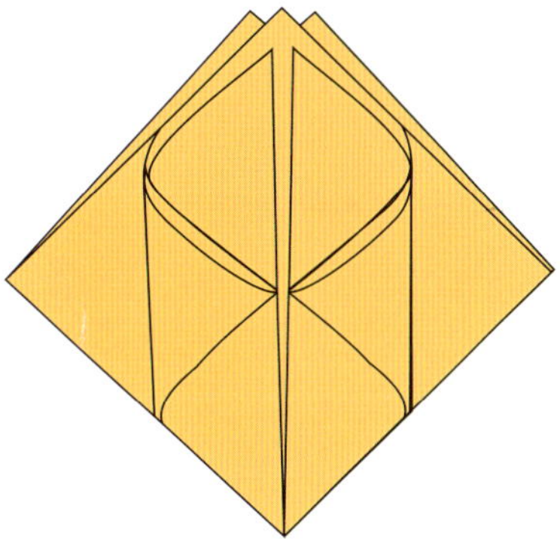

13 ....like this.

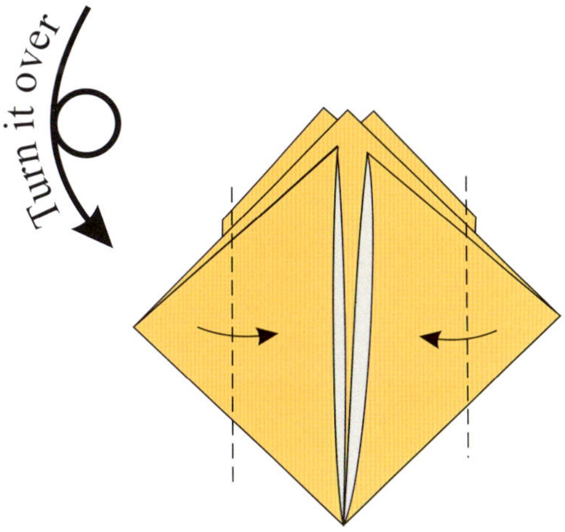

14 Again fold the right and the left corners inside as you did in step no.12.

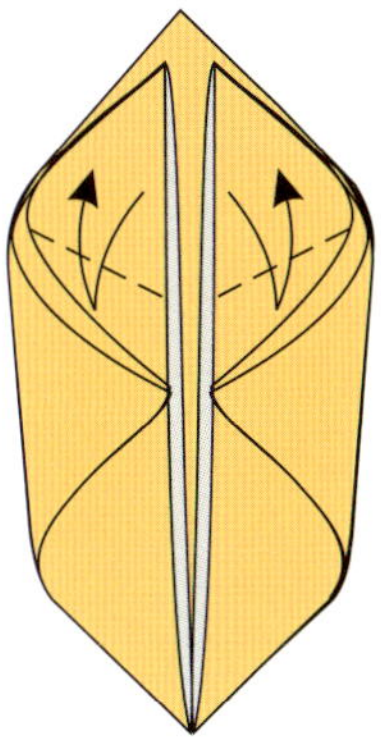

15 Your form will look like this. Now, fold both the top front flaps downwards along the dotted lines, make creases and unfold them.

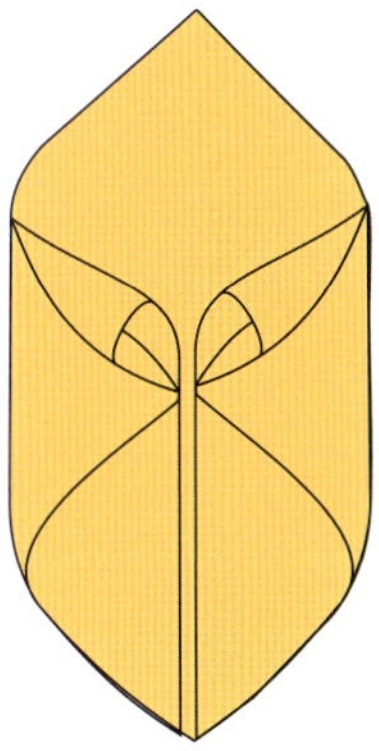

16 Now, tuck both the top flaps in to the triangular pockets as shown. To do this open the triangular pockets with your fingers and slip the top corners deep inside.

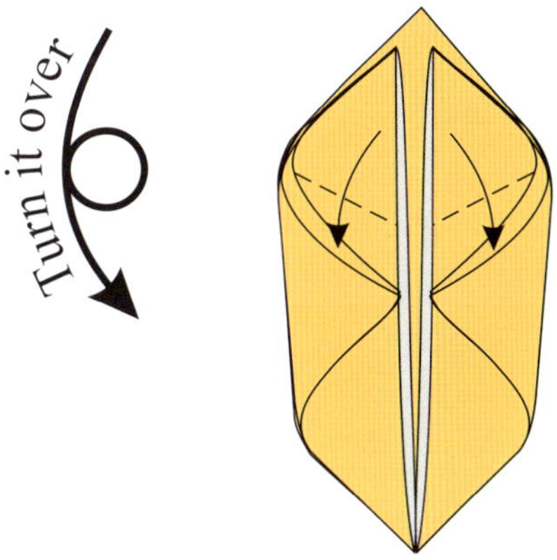

17 Repeat step nos. 15 and 16 with this side also.

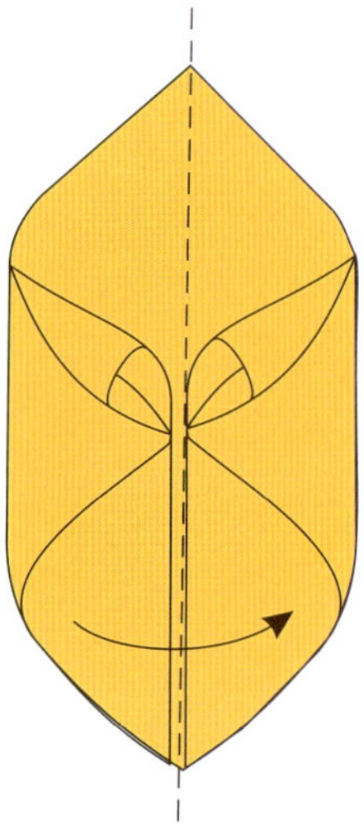

18 Fold the left half of the upper flap along the dotted line so that it overlaps the right half. Repeat the same step with the back side also

19 Your form will look like this.

20 Blow up the balloon through the bottom hole.

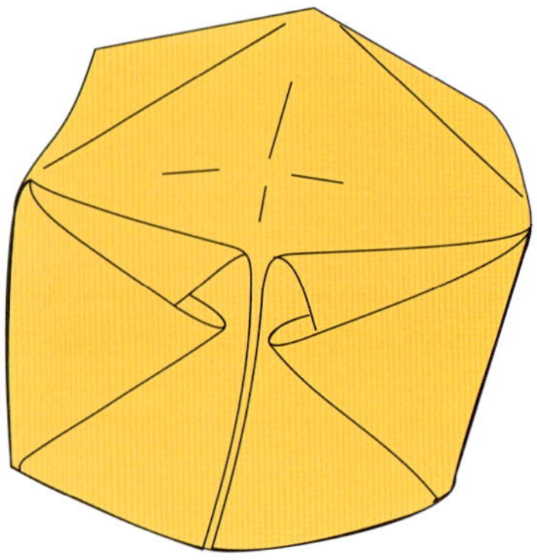

21 Your balloon is ready.

Collage Work

Animal Head

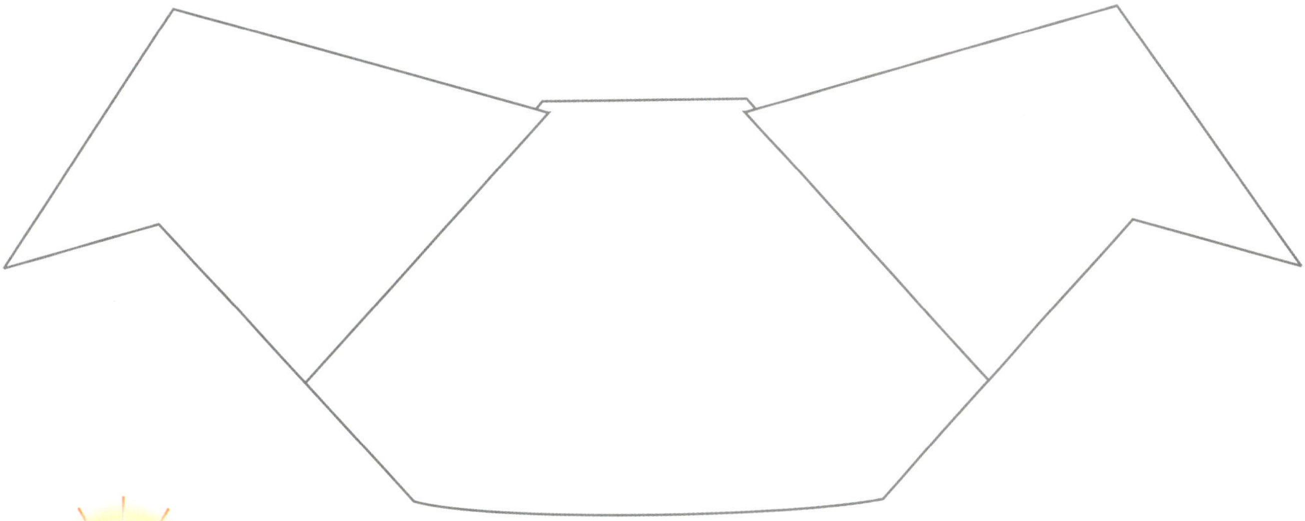

TIPS AND TRICKS

Step-1 Collect paper sheets of various colours of your own choice. Tear them in small pieces of different shapes.

Step-2 Set them within the outline and paste in the given shape.

Cut and Paste

Lady Bird

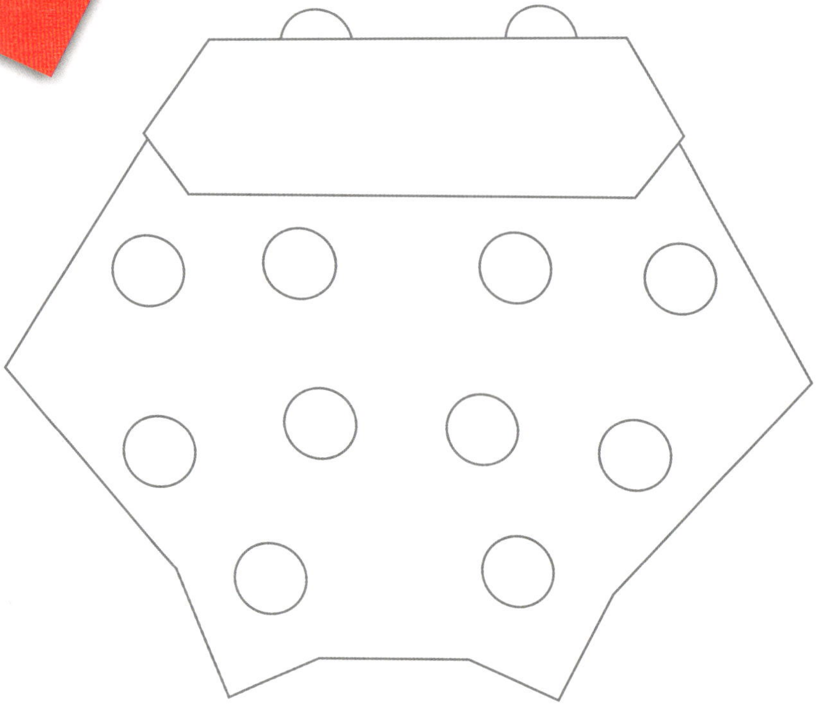

TIPS AND TRICKS

Step-1 Take craft paper sheets of various colours. Trace different parts on the shape of different colours.

Step-2 Now paste these pieces at the appropriate places.

Crushed Paper Art

Talking Crow

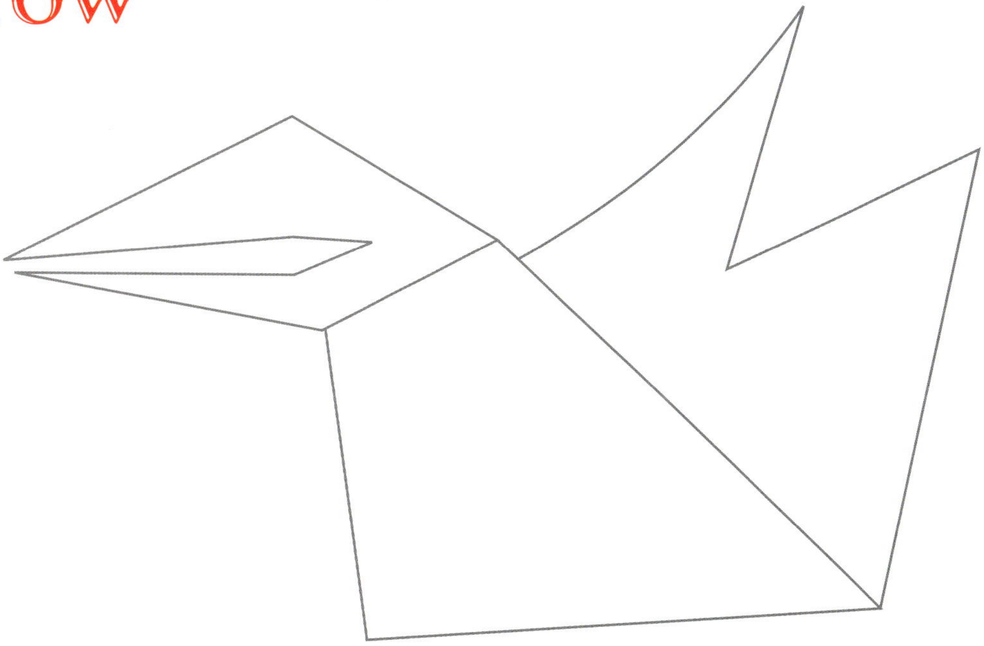

TIPS AND TRICKS

Step-1 Take a plain paper and squeeze it in your hand. Open it gently and apply the poster colour with a flat brush.

Step-2 Now cut the paper according to the shape and paste it within the outline.

Spray Paint

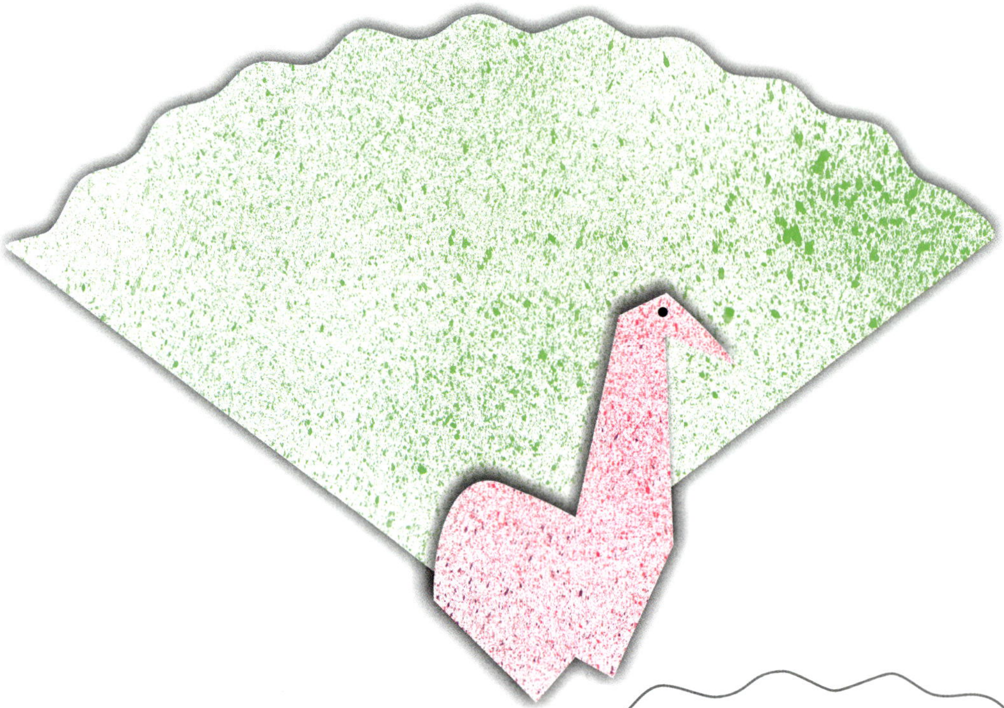

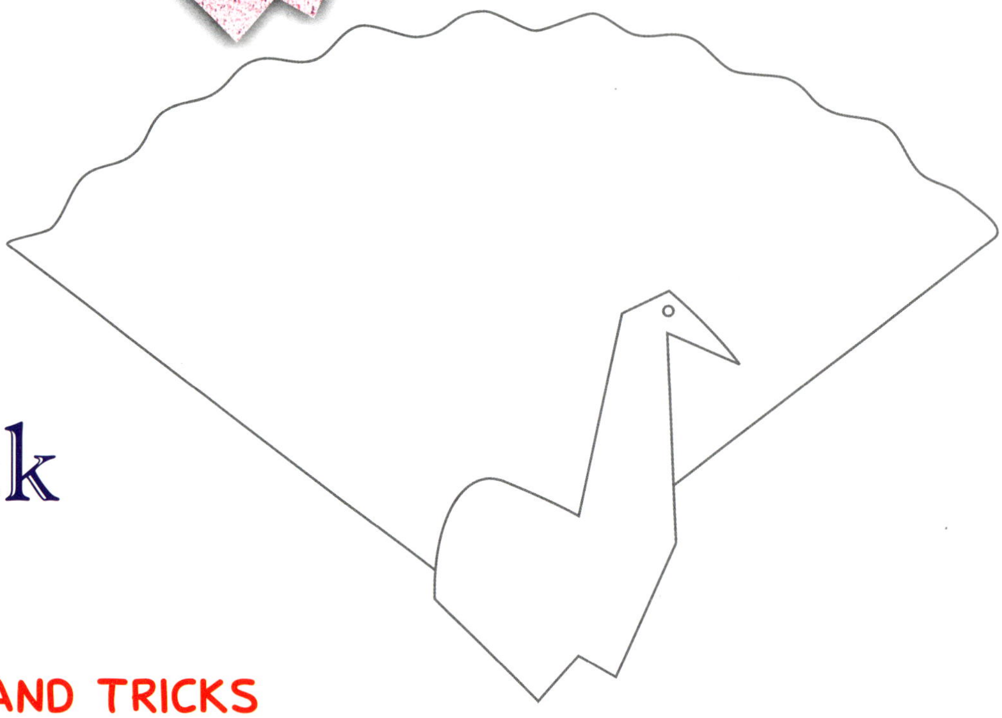

Peacock

TIPS AND TRICKS

Step-1 Take a white paper. Spray different colours of your own choice with a tooth brush on the white paper.

Step-2 Cut the parts of the shape as per your liking and paste them on the figure.